Prime Time

Physical

A movement approach to learning and development

Jo Blank

Contents

Published by Practical Pre-School Books, A Division of MA Education Ltd, St Jude's Church, Dulwich Road, Herne Hill, London, SE24 0PB.

Tel: 020 7738 5454 www.practicalpreschoolbooks.com

Associate Publisher: Angela Morano Shaw

Design: Alison Coombes **fonthill**creative 01722 717043

All images © MA Education Ltd 2016.

Introduction

The national picture

The importance of healthy physical development is recognised in recent national reports, and in the revised EYFS (2012) where it is defined as a 'prime area'. Concerns about childhood obesity have prompted national guidelines on the amount and type of physical activity children under 5 should be doing (Start Active, Stay Active, 2011). These Factsheets can be found at www.gov.uk/government/publications/uk=physical-activity-guidelines

> *"regular physical activity in the early years provides immediate and long-term benefits for physical and psychological well-being."*
> (Start Active, Stay Active, 2011)

More recently, a manifesto for physical activity in the early years has been published, ('The Best Start in Life', 2016). It states that 91% of children aged 2-4 years in the UK are not active enough to be healthy. It calls for the government to embed more physical activity into national early years policy, ensuring that high levels of activity are supported at home, in settings and within the wider community. It demands:

> *"Greater emphasis on the importance of physical activity across the Early Years Foundation Stage curriculum, alongside clear guidance and training for early years practitioners on how to promote and develop children's physical activity."*

This book aims to do just that.

About this book

The main purpose of **Prime Time Physical** is to ensure that children get the exercise they need for healthy development and the motivation to lead healthy lifestyles. This can be described as 'Physical Literacy', *'the motivation, confidence, physical competence, knowledge and understanding to value and take responsibility for engagement in physical activities for life'* (Whitehead, 2014). **Prime Time Physical** champions a physical approach to the EYFS, making the most of children's natural desire to be active.

Young children love to move and find out what their bodies can do. A key role for early years practitioners is to capitalise on this joy of movement, and help children to gain control and feel good in their bodies. This book is all about adults providing the support and environment for children to become competent and confident movers and learners.

> 'A child's experience of movement will play a pivotal part in shaping his personality, his feelings, and his achievements.' (Sally Goddard Blythe, 2004)

There are examples throughout the book of how to provide a 'movement friendly' environment, and high quality movement experiences for children of all ages.

The four main sections of the book cover all the different ways physical activities are presented to children. The first is about natural developmental movement promoted through movement play (based on the work of Jabadao, 2007). The second progresses to developing specific movement skills through fun games, and the third describes how movement and dance help children to develop an awareness of how and where the body moves. The final section, covering movement and the Curriculum, focuses on making learning physical across all areas, to build on children's natural exuberance and fuel their desire to learn.

The aim of the 8-week programme is to embed a physical approach to learning in your setting. It takes you, the practitioner, through a step-by-step development process, to increase your knowledge and understanding, and enable you to provide vibrant and fun physical experiences for all children every day.

The body and the brain

How the body works

Exercise helps the functioning of the cardiovascular and muscular systems, and strengthens the bones.

Understanding how the body works when we exercise is central to providing movement experiences for children. This knowledge can be shared with children as they grow, to help them learn why they need to be active and the importance of an active lifestyle.

How does the body work? We breathe and take in oxygen through the nose and mouth, this travels through the lungs, and into the blood stream. The heart pumps the blood around the body and sends oxygen to the muscles so they can work hard.

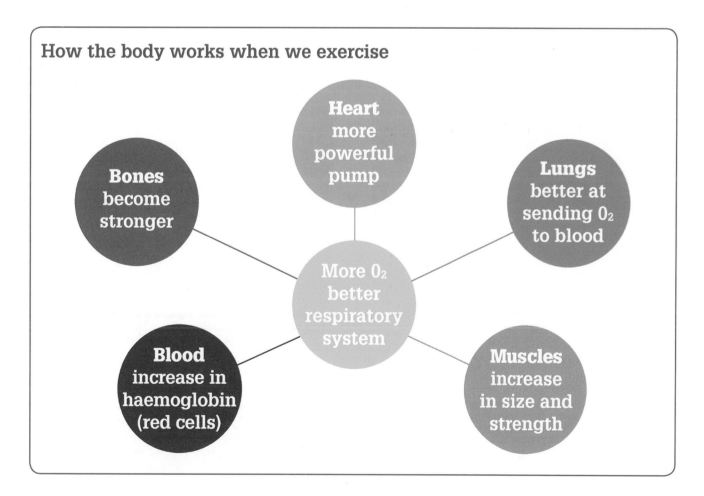

How the body works when we exercise

- **Heart** more powerful pump
- **Lungs** better at sending O_2 to blood
- **Bones** become stronger
- **Muscles** increase in size and strength
- **Blood** increase in haemoglobin (red cells)
- **More O_2 better respiratory system**

Development Matters emphasises the importance of free movement play:

- 'Help babies to become aware of their own bodies through touch and movement' (Birth-11 months)
- 'Moves freely and with pleasure and confidence' (30-50 months).
- 'Young children explore particular patterns of movement' (16-26 months).
- 'Support and encourage babies' drive to stand and walk'(8-20 months).

So what happens in the body when you exercise? The lungs get more efficient at sending oxygen into the bloodstream; the harder you exercise, the harder the heart works to pump oxygen around the body, and so the heart gets stronger. As muscles work harder, they demand and use more oxygen, which in turn makes the muscles stronger and faster. The whole process improves the efficiency of the respiratory system. Weight bearing activities are essential for strengthening the bones.

There is a simple exercise routine for 2-5s (p 34) that is a fun way to help children to understand how their bodies work.

Movement builds the brain

Movement builds the brain and vice versa, by moving we learn.

All learning comes through the senses, and the central nervous system sends messages to the brain. The body responds through movement; this is called the sensory-motor system. This system remains throughout life and all other brain functions develop from this. So, after learning through direct contact with the environment (babies reaching out and touching and exploring things) we develop our ability to think abstractly (Piaget). As practitioners, we need to remember that the sensory-motor system is dominant in young children. The foundations for learning are crucially developed during the first three and a half years of life.

The movement patterns that babies go through (sitting up, crawling, etc.) have to be fully completed before the next one can begin. Pushing babies on too soon to their next phase may result in something not developing in the body or connecting in the brain. Sit-in baby walkers, for example, may reduce time for valuable floor play and place undue pressure on toes. Tummy and back play will develop their muscles ready for sitting, and develop key areas of the brain. Crawling strengthens hips, the trunk, shoulders, arms and hands, not only in preparation for upright movement but for learning, as crawling prompts vital connections between both sides of the brain.

'The movement of the body activates the motor cortex in the brain, which in turn prompts further complex movements of the body, so babies go from belly wriggling to crawling, sitting up, standing and finally walking.' (Carla Hannaford, 1995)

Section 1: Movement Play

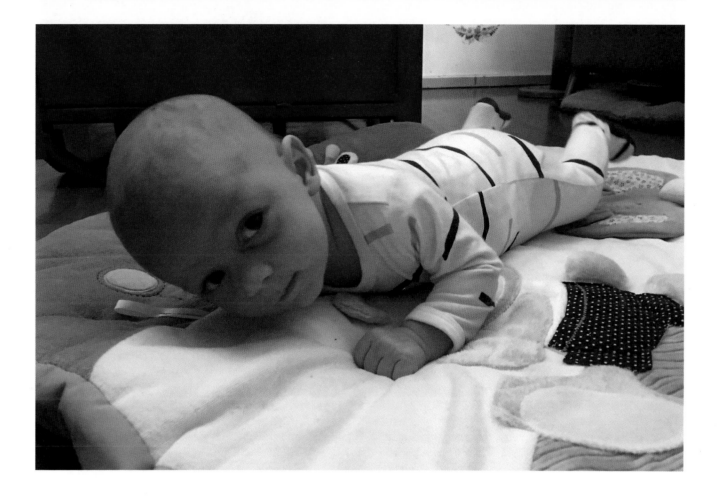

Why is it important?

This section is about promoting children's natural physical development. It explains how 'movement play' (based on Jabadao, 2007) enables them to explore what their bodies can do, is essential for brain development and helps them to become who they are.

Given the right environment and adult support, babies and young children naturally seek to practise and develop movements that are right for them at the time. Their bodies know what they need to do!

These movements prompt brain development and form the basis for developing more complex physical skills.

Movement is the natural way children learn. Babies and children use their bodies to learn how they fit into the world. Early movement play builds essential skills for life. Movement play is ordinary playful movement based on

children's natural developmental movement. It is child-led and is about exploring what the body can do.

Developmental movement is children's natural physical development. It is the sequence of reflexes and movement patterns that begin at birth and continue through childhood that help our bodies work efficiently. Examples are grasping, flinging arms back (reflexes), rolling, spinning, crawling, running (movement patterns).

All humans are born with reflexes and some develop after birth. These are instinctive responses to stimuli. Some are necessary for survival, like the moro reflex. This is when a baby throws back their arms in a response to a sudden noise, or lowering of the head. Given enough opportunity to move their bodies, babies and toddlers gradually gain control over these spontaneous reflexes. The moro reflex is usually integrated by four months.

Development Matters emphasises the importance of equipment and the environment:

- 'Provide different arrangements of toys and soft play materials to encourage crawling, tumbling, rolling and climbing' (16-26 months).
- 'Let babies kick and stretch freely on their tummies and backs' (birth-11months).

For some children, certain reflexes are still present in later life, and may affect posture, balance, and coordination. This is likely to create anxiety, which could, in turn, affect behaviour. Repeated, natural movements will ensure continued healthy development. The more a child moves, the better his control over his reflexes becomes. (Sally Goddard Blythe, 2004)

Movement patterns are those movements that all children go through as they grow and mature, for example, rolling over, sitting up, crawling, walking, jumping etc. The patterns developing from around 3 years, where children are focusing more on specific body parts, are also known as movement skills. Given space, encouragement and motivation the early movement patterns will happen naturally. As children grow and begin to develop their movement skills, they need both freedom to explore and focused support and teaching (see Section 2).

It may be that some children with physical disabilities, learning difficulties, or behaviour concerns, may not have had sufficient movement experience to integrate their reflexes, or they may not have completed their natural movement patterns. For example, babies may have been carried constantly in chairs, with no floor play. A poor diet of early movement experiences could affect children's balance, co-ordination, anxiety, and eye tracking. (Sally Goddard Blythe, 2004)

By enabling children to go through these early movement patterns at a later stage, the brain and body have further opportunities to develop those connections not already made.

Developmental movement is biologically embedded; it happens naturally, but it happens in response to stimulation of the senses. Children have an inner drive to explore the world through movement and it is up to practitioners to enable children to respond to this instinct for sensory motor experience by providing the right environment, resources, encouragement and stimulation.

As children explore their own ways of moving, they prompt the building of their bodies (bones, muscles, organs, connective tissue) and the building of connections in their nervous systems and brains. Movement builds bodies and brains! (Greenland, 2000)

Key movement activities

The Jabadao organisation has identified 5 key movement activities that are essential for all children, to help them grow and develop healthily. These activities will ensure that the essential reflexes and movement patterns are fully developed. (Jabadao, 2007)

Babies and children of all ages need:

- Floor play on backs & tummies

- Belly crawling & wriggling play

- Crawling

- Spinning, tipping, rolling, falling play

- Pushing, pulling, stretching, hanging and buffeting about play.

The Department of Health physical activity guidelines (2011, updated 2016) recognise the importance of these activities, recommending lots of 'tummy time' for infants who are not yet walking and lots of 'energetic bouts of activity' for children capable of walking.

A challenging environment and knowledgeable, positive and enthusiastic practitioners are essential ingredients for a successful physical play programme.

These key movements are essential for children to practise, because they not only develop basic movement skills, but the senses for balance and bodily awareness: the proprioceptive and vestibular senses.

Reflection

How well do you know children's stages of physical development? Check Development Matters for the age range you care for.

How well do you focus on the physical skills children are practising now, and what they are trying to achieve?

Observe children in your key group. Identify and record their stage of development, the movement patterns they are practising, and what they are likely to do next.

Proprioceptive development

Proprioception is the felt sense of body. It lets us know where our bodies are in relation to space and the environment. It is the information gained through receptors in the muscles (proprioceptors) as we come into contact with things. Proprioception helps us learn about the force of movements. For example, it is the sense that enables us to decide how much force to use to kick a ball a long or short distance. Proprioception leads to the development of balance.

Vestibular development

The vestibular sense is vitally important. It is about the body's relationship to gravity and the ground and underpins balance. It monitors the movements of our head and stabilises the eyes in relation to the environment. The eyes must stay in a stable position in relation to the ground. It is only through movement that our sense of balance develops.

We know that gentle rocking movements have a calming effect, as in rocking a baby to sleep, and that rapid movement increases excitement, as in throwing the child in the air, rough and tumble, roundabouts and swings. All these actions help develop their sense of balance. (Jabadao)

Children need experiences moving in different places:

■ Up and down – jumping, trampolining, sliding

■ To and fro – running, swinging

■ Round and round – roundabouts

■ Turning movements of the body – spinning, twirling, rolling, somersaulting

■ From side to side – off balance, for example, Wobble Board.

The inner ear canals work like a 'spirit level' to maintain a feeling of balance when the body turns upside down and spins etc.

All these experiences work the balance mechanism and develop it. Young children do not get dizzy like adults do, because the connections between balance and other centres, like the eyes, are still being formed before the age of 8 (Sally Goddard Blythe, 2004).

Reflection

How well do you provide for the 5 key movement activities? Write down the equipment and activities available in your nursery to promote this type of play.

How well do you provide for the different balance activities that prompt vestibular development?

The adult role

Developing positive attitudes

Children must develop positive attitudes towards physical activity and have fun being active if they are to become healthy active people. Children learn attitudes from the people they spend time with and the experiences they have both inside and outside the home. Practitioners are essential role models and attitude counts!

> *"The seeds of low level activity are laid down at a very early age"* (Armstrong, 1982)

Reflection

Be conscious of what you say throughout the day, and write it down. Ask a colleague to tell you when they hear you commenting on children's spontaneous movements.

Think about what you say to children during the day. Do you say things such as:

'Take care you might fall!'
'Don't run!'
'Don't climb too high!'
'Stop jumping up and down!'
'Stop being silly' (when rolling around the floor for example)
'Stop doing that you'll make yourself dizzy!'

Think how these comments affect children's attitudes to being active, exploring what their bodies can do, trying out new things and taking risks.

Read the following extracts (taken from the book *Hopping Home Backwards*, Penny Greenland, 2000) to see how differently the practitioners respond to children's spontaneous movements.

Nursery 1

It is time for a story and Mrs Stone asks the children to come and sit on the carpet. 'Hurry up!' she calls. 'Quickly, quickly, sit on the carpet, legs crossed, nice straight backs.' The children come to the carpet in all different ways that reflect how they are feeling this morning. Rashid flies in all jumps and bounds; Morag slithers slowly, scuffing the toes of her shoes along the floor. Ned turns circles as he goes and arrives dizzy and unfocussed. Martin sits down with his legs out in front of him. 'Come along. Walk properly everyone. Cross your legs Martin,' I don't like sitting with my legs crossed', Martin complains. 'It hurts!' There isn't much space here', says Mrs Stone. 'We all need to cross our legs so that we can make room for the person next to us.'

Nursery 2

As the children arrive for the start of the day Mrs Cole asks them to come and sit on the carpet. "Let's see how you are arriving today" she says. "Jo and Fiona are walking together, Dan is hopping with his arms out and Jamila is going as slow as possible...it'll take a long time to get right across to the carpet! Dean is going round and round. He'll have to walk further than everyone else to get to the same place!" When most of the children have sat down (and Jamila is delighting in taking as long as possible) Mrs Cole says, "Look around at all the different ways we are sitting... all the different shapes we are making with our bodies. What can you see?" After they have spent time practising their movement observation skills Mrs Cole says, "Right. Get comfortable everyone. Make sure you're not taking up the space that belongs to the person next to you, and change from looking to listening".

Consider ways of responding positively to children about the movements they do. The EYFS emphasises the importance of talking about movement.

Development Matters emphasises the importance of music and movement:

- 'Talk to children about their movements and help them to explore new ways of moving' (22-36 months).
- 'Encourage children to use the vocabulary of movement' (30-50 months).
- 'Provide CD players, scarves, streamers and musical instruments so that children can respond spontaneously to music'(8-20 months).

Ask questions and make comments such as:

- How does that feel when you spin round and round?

- How can you get up there without your knees touching?

- Look at your body twisting round! What shape is it making?

- I can see you are using your knees then your hands then turning your whole body over

- You look lively today! Let's go outside to run around.

Supporting Movement Play

Your role is to:

- Provide a movement friendly environment (see next section)

- Notice and value what children do, and talk about it

- Join in their play if they want you to

- Notice how children choose to move, observe and record

- Help children with their vocabulary for their movement, use simple language to describe what you see

- Encourage movement through interactions, copying, following the child's lead.

Get active!

Providing a movement friendly environment

Why? Children are naturally driven to do these significant movements at any time, and the best support you can provide is an appropriate movement friendly environment.

Resources: Equipment that supports early movement, like tunnels, body balls, rockers, soft play, climbing equipment, a soft surface, cushions, tummy rolls.

How?

- Provide sufficient clear floor space; ensure adults are at floor level
- Place some toys and equipment on the floor
- Value floor based movement even if children can walk
- Enable children to choose how they sit at certain times of the day, such as story time
- Use belly crawling or crawling in familiar games, such as 'What time is it Mr Wolf?'
- Have fun moving from one place to another during routines: march to go outside, be aeroplanes to get to the snack table.

Helpful hint: Value movement learning by talking about it and making it visible on displays and in learning journeys.

Setting up a movement area

Why? A movement area values movement in your room and makes it of equal importance to other learning areas. Just as you organise role play, construction and writing areas, you can provide an area for movement. It provides a place for children just to 'be', to move when they want to, and to explore strong feelings when needed. A movement area can be permanent or available for part of the week, if there are space issues.

Resources: A floor space with surfaces for sliding, rolling, dancing and relaxing. Props to encourage different movements, such as ribbon sticks, scarves, musical instruments, hoops, elastics, Lycra, soft body balls. For younger children, textured materials to encourage touching and feeling such as pine cones, brushes, sponges, massage balls, bark and peat. These could be put into trays for crawling and walking on. Use different textured carpet squares for crawling and walking on. An easy to use CD player, a collection of music to create different moods and stimulate a range of movements: slow, fast, peaceful, lively (Arc Music, World Music series).

How? As with any new area, children will need help as they discover how to use this area and keep themselves and each other safe. Talk about the things you can do in the movement area such as rolling around, relaxing, dancing, playing with others, boisterous play. The rules they must remember are:

- Don't hurt yourself
- Don't hurt anyone else (Jabadao, 2007).

Enable children to take responsibility for their own safety, by helping them to notice what is risky. Encourage children to ask for help if they need it. If a child is moving in a way that concerns you, stop the activity and help them notice the risks, consider the possible consequences and find solutions.

Helpful hint: Place some drawing materials in the area sometimes, so that children can express themselves in art, whilst relaxing and listening to music.

Pizza massage

Why? This is a lovely relaxing and calming activity. It can help children to be comfortable with appropriate touch, and develop their proprioception and sensitivity.

Resources: A comfortable place, a soft ball to roll on the backs of children who are wary of personal contact.

How? Massage a child's back as they lie on their tummy.
1. Always ask the child for their permission to do a pizza massage
2. Knead the dough gently with your fingers
3. Spread on the tomato paste with the palms of your hands
4. Ask the child what they would like on their pizza, ham, mushrooms, tomatoes, sweetcorn, etc. and pretend to put this all over, with gentle presses
5. Sprinkle cheese all over with gentle finger play
6. Cut the pizza into slices using the side of your hand in criss-cross motion.

Helpful hint: Children can give each other a pizza massage. Use a soft ball for the massage if children feel more comfortable.

This massage could develop into any sort of food, for example, mashed potato, sausages, chips, pasta, ice cream.

Weather massage

1. The sun is shining; make circular movements with flat hands all over the back
2. It begins to rain; make raindrops with gentle finger play, faster, then slower as it gradually stops
3. The thunder rumbles; massage all over the back
4. Lightning strikes; slide the side of the hand across the back in different directions
5. It rains again, pitter patter
6. The sun comes out again; make circular movements with flat hands
7. A rainbow comes out; make a big arc over the back, sweeping the hands from one side to the other.

Animal massage

Pretend different animals are walking on your back.

1. A mouse is slowly creeping over your back
2. A wiggly worm sildes around
3. A cat or a dog
4. An elephant or a dinosaur.

Helpful hint: Ask the child which animal they would like, whether they are fast, slow, light or heavy. Ask the child if they would like to give you a massage; encourage them to use the same language and to ask you questions.

Get active!

Why? Adult-initiated activities are a way to encourage children's significant movements in a more structured but open-ended way.

1. Activity circuits

Resources: A range of large physical play equipment, including tunnels, steps, climbing frame, slide, netting, balance beams, and a range of small equipment such as hoops, cones and bean bags.

How? Create a circuit using equipment that encourages a variety of different movements, for example, belly crawling under netting, crawling through a tunnel, rolling down a slope, sliding backwards and forwards along a bench. Encourage movements on the tummy and back.

Helpful hint: Enable children to create their own challenging circuits by organising the equipment differently. Encourage them to find their own ingenious ways of moving, on their tummies and backs and by rolling.

Describe what they are doing with their bodies as they move. Give them challenges such as, 'can you move along there without putting your feet down?' 'Can you move along the balance equipment sideways?'.

2. Activity games

Focus on significant movement activities and skills.

3. Movement sessions

Focus on the 5 key movement experiences.
Pretend to be animals and use the floor to be crocodiles. worms and snakes.

Helpful hint: Play active games (Section 2) every day and make them as important as other activities.

Get active!

'...the beginning of upright balance starts on the tummy.' (Sally Goddard Blythe, 2004)

Activity 1: Floor play on back

Why? Back play is essential for healthy development. It develops children's proprioception and helps them develop a sense of self as they feel their whole body in contact with the ground. They can find their toes and fingers and strengthen their core muscles.

Resources: You, the practitioner! A comfortable place to lie, overhead activity things to reach and touch.

How? Finding the fingers and toes
- Use different kinds of pressure on baby's bare feet with your fingers; blow on them etc.
- Play games that introduce toes and fingers to each other, make up rhymes such as: 'hello toes, hello toes, hello fingers, hello fingers, hold your toes touch your nose', etc. and encourage babies to find their own feet
- Use music to move legs and arms gently in rhythm
- Sing Incy Wincy spider and do the actions moving baby's arms and legs, letting your fingers crawl from their feet to their face
- Play round and round the garden with feet as well as hands
- Gently rock and roll the baby around like a ball as they hold their feet
- Child curls up tightly and adult gently tries to uncurl them. Let the older toddler do it to the adult too.

Reach and grasp
Encourage babies to reach out and grasp objects you hold, sometimes hold on to the object and encourage gentle pulling, place toys and objects to the side to encourage turning and rolling. Use balloons for them to touch and bubbles to watch and reach.

Reflex – Tonic neck pattern
Put very young babies on their back and watch this pattern emerge. A young baby will face their extended arm when first on their back. They are biologically programmed to develop their distance vision by looking at their own extended finger. So watch for the classic position, one arm extended, often with pointy finger, the head facing the same way, the other elbow bent with the hand at about ear height. The legs will move if the position changes sides. Play games to encourage babies to change their focus from one side to another and watch the pattern in their arms and legs.

Activity 2: Floor play on tummy

Why? Tummy play is essential for healthy development. It develops children's proprioception and helps them develop a sense of self as they feel their whole body in contact with the ground. It strengthens the neck, head, shoulders and spine and prepares the body for crawling and walking.

Resources: A comfortable floor surface, sometimes a mat/blanket children can grasp to help them move forwards, toys and objects to reach, and most importantly you, the practitioner.

How? Head lifting and pushing up
- Give babies plenty of time on their tummies, time to drift and settle into this position
- Get down on the floor and stare and talk to each other to encourage them to lift their heads; talk to them on different sides
- Use small toys and objects for them to watch and reach.

If babies don't like being on their tummies (and they often don't) use soft comforting props to bring their 'tummy centre' to their attention (lying on cushions, a body roll, body ball etc). Lie babies on your tummy and chest. Build up their tolerance gradually.

On the tummy and moving! Encourage babies to push and pull themselves with their feet, knees and hands, it is natural for their bodies to do this. Encourage them to move around in a circle on a smooth floor surface.

Helpful hint: Stroke the baby's hands to open and strengthen them.

Get active!

Activity 3: Belly crawling and crawling

Why? Belly crawling and crawling are essential for healthy development. They develop critical brain connections, strengthen legs, hips, shoulders and spine. The head lifts to practise eye tracking, in preparation for reading. The hands open to enable smooth movement.

Resources: Toys to move towards, different low level steps and surfaces, tunnels, material to crawl under.

How?
- Create different low level surfaces to negotiate and feel
- Get down on the floor and playfully mirror their movements
- Have races, chase them, squirming and crawling, play Peek-a-boo
- Play bridges by crawling through each other's legs on all fours
- Use a blanket, parachute or Lycra to crawl underneath, and tunnels to crawl through
- Reach for toys, chase balls and cars
- Pretend to be crocodiles and snakes
- Sing rhymes like 'Wiggly Woo' and squirm on tummy like a worm, sing 'Five Little Ducks' and swim on tummies.

Helpful hint: Notice children's different developmental stages as they begin to belly crawl and crawl. Some children may not crawl, but bottom shuffle or roll instead; this is perfectly normal development. Even if children are bottom shuffling, or rolling, still put them on their tummies to strengthen their neck, shoulders, spine and arms.

Activity 4: Spinning and tipping

Why? Spinning and tipping are essential for healthy development of the vestibular system. This is vital to develop our relationship with gravity and the ground. Children naturally seek 'off balance' activities like spinning and tilting to stimulate their vestibular system.

Resources: Lycra for rocking babies in, music, scarves, ribbon sticks and pom poms for dancing.

How?
- Use Lycra to rock and spin babies in with 2 adults
- Play upside down, rocking and swinging games like aeroplanes, let them climb up your body and turn over
- Let them spin, play music and twirl then pretend to fall down
- Dance and twirl with babies and toddlers in your arms
- Sing rhymes that involve spinning (Teddy Bear Teddy Bear turn around)
- Play seesaw, row the boat, Hickory Dickory Dock with a side to side 'tick tock' movement, Humpty Dumpty when they fall through your legs.

Activity 5: Exciting surfaces and circuits

Why? To encourage crawling and exploration.

Resources: Create different surfaces to crawl on, such as bubble wrap, soft furry material, sponge, paper, wood, carpet etc. Create a slope to crawl up, humps to crawl over with cushions, use tunnels to crawl through and create tunnels with material and chairs.

How? Encourage babies to crawl on these different surfaces, or lie on their tummies and feel the different textures. Crawl alongside them around the circuit.

Activity 6: Crawling bean bags

Why? To encourage crawling.

Resources: Bean bags.

How? Put a bean bag on the child's back and encourage them to crawl keeping it on their back, have a race with them!

Helpful hint: Let them follow you or each other and pick up the bean bag when it falls off.

Activity 7: Musical bumps

Why? This encourages free movement and expression, develops a feeling for rhythm and is fun!

Resources: Lively music and space.

How? Dance around and when the music stops, all sit down; get up and dance when it begins again.

Helpful hint: This could develop into musical statues.

Activity 8: Balloon fun

Why? This will help children explore force and motion, it gets them moving and reaching and is fun!

Resources: Balloons and string.

How? Attach a line of balloons to string and suspend them so children can stretch or jump to reach them. Let children run through the balloons and bat them. Suspend them lower for lying babies, perhaps on a pole between chairs.

Helpful hint: Let them walk through them batting them with just their heads. Bat a balloon between you encouraging hand-eye coordination.

Activity 9: Let's walk like...

Why? This encourages body tension, explores use of weight, speed and different levels and gets them on their backs and tummies.

Resources: Different types of music and space!

How? Pretend to be...elephants, lions, rabbits, mice, snakes, crocodiles etc. and move like they do.

Helpful hint: Let the toddler decide on the animal and you follow their lead.

Section 2: Movement Skills

Why is it important?

Basic movement skills are the movement patterns a child is physically ready to develop and refine between the ages of 3 and 5 years and are about using different body parts. Young children need to develop their basic movement skills in the early years so they can develop more complex skills later. To perform skills in sports, children need to combine their basic skills. So, for example, in football, they combine the separate skills of running and kicking as they pass and shoot; in basketball and netball, they combine jumping with throwing and catching, as they pluck a ball from the air and shoot at goal.

Children can develop their basic movement skills by the age of five and perform them competently by the age of seven (Gallahue, 1982), so it is crucial to help children learn these skills or movement patterns in the EYFS. They are the foundation movements for their future sports and physical recreation.

Not mastering basic movement patterns leads to reduced potential for learning more advanced skills. (Gallahue, 1982).

You see children naturally practising many of these basic skills every day, given the space and equipment. Careful planning and teaching will ensure all children get the chance to develop the full range of foundation skills to build on in the future.

Reflection

Which skills do children practise in your nursery? What activities do you do to develop these skills? List the skills that are frequently practised, and those that are least practised.

Basic Movement Skills (what the body does)

Basic movement skills are the movements a child is physically ready to develop and refine during the early years.

LOCOMOTOR SKILLS Moving from A to B	BALANCE SKILLS Balancing the body in stillness and in motion	BALL SKILLS Send, receive, travel, strike
Crawling Running Galloping Walking Hopping Skipping Dodging	Rolling Stopping Bending Twisting Landing Stretching Climbing Static and dynamic balancing Turning Swinging	Throwing Catching Striking Bouncing Dribbling Kicking

Basic movement skills (patterns) can be grouped into:

Locomotor skills: used to move the body from one place to another. These include walking, running, skipping, hopping, jumping, sliding, leaping, climbing.

Balance skills: used to control the body when still. These include, bending, stretching, twisting and turning.

Ball skills: used to send an object, receive an object and travel with an object. These include throwing, rolling, catching, kicking, dribbling, striking.

How do children develop their basic movement skills?

To develop any skill, at any age, the process is the same.

There are 3 phases of skill development:

DISCOVERING PHASE
(exploration and experimentation)
This is when you try out something new, in a variety of ways, experimenting to find out the best way to succeed.

DEVELOPING PHASE
(practise and modify)
This is when you realise how it should be done and keep trying and improving. You work out which muscles are needed for the skill to work, and which muscles you can relax.

CONSOLIDATING PHASE
(well-coordinated and purposeful)
This is when you have succeeded in performing the skill well, using all the right muscles and using it as a means to an end. You enjoy repeating the skill and seek more difficulty.

Development Matters emphasises the importance of developing movement skills:

- 'Slithering, shuffling, rolling, crawling, walking, running, jumping, skipping, sliding and hopping' (30-50 months).
- 'Shows increasing control over an object in pushing, patting, throwing, catching and kicking it' (40-60 months).

The adult role

It is highly dependent on the adult to provide the right environment and support at the right time for the skill to develop successfully. Each movement pattern/skill goes through the same process of development, from the discovering phase, through the practising phase, to the consolidating phase.

"The quality of instruction given to children is perhaps the most crucial factor influencing the development of their movement skills." (Gallahue, 1996)

Reflection

How much do you notice the different stages of children's skill development?
Take some time to observe children's movements and decide on their stages of development.
Consider the type of interaction that would help them best.

The adult role

Adult role during discovering stage	• Lots of space • Intuitive adults, who make appropriate comments and provide equipment at the right time • Encouragement and enthusiasm • Praise
Adult role during developing phase	• Praise, notice the small improvements! • Accurate observations • Suggestions for improvement • Appropriate teaching points • Patience!
Adult role during consolidating phase	• Praise and recognition • Additional challenges • Knowledge of the next stage • A purpose

Get active!

Locomotor and balance skills for 2-5s

Activity 1: Hoop play

Why? Using hoops is a fun way to develop the basic skills of jumping, hopping and balancing through a playful, problem solving approach.

Resources: A hoop for each child and for you and space!

How? Give challenges!
- Jump in and out, 2 feet to 2 feet, 1 foot to the other foot, 1 foot to the same foot (hop)
- Jump in and out sideways, backwards and forwards
- Leap over it – a more challenging jump!
- Put feet inside and walk hands around the outside, and vice versa
- Put bottom inside and 1 foot and 1 hand outside, play around doing this with different body parts
- Give open-ended challenges, such as put 3 parts of your body inside and 1 outside
- Balance on 2 parts of your body inside the hoop
- Pretend it's a puddle and stamp and splash in it, jump over it
- Take your whole body through the hoop and jump through it (like a skipping rope).

- With a partner, one holding the hoop, find different ways of getting through it on hands and feet, back, tummy.

Helpful hint: Ask questions that all children can interpret in their own way, including children who are physically challenged.

Activity 2: Lifeboats

Why? It is a fast-paced fun game for a large group that enables children to practise their basic skills of running and stopping, dodging, and using their body in different ways, and also to respond to clear movement instructions and develop their vocabulary!

Resources: Spots, hoops, carpet squares, or some type of non-slip markers.

How? Spread out the markers around the space, one for each child. Explain that the game is set at sea and they are all on a big ship. They are the sailors and have to follow the instructions of the captain (you). They do different movements to each instruction.

Lifeboats = all stand on marker/hoop, these are their lifeboats that are all on the big ship and they can jump into any of them once the game starts. Explain the sides of the room/area are the front, back and sides of the big ship:
Port = left
Starboard = right
Bow = front

Stern = back
Just use 2 instructions to begin with and when you shout these words they can run to the correct side of the room.
Climb the ladder = pretend to climb ladder
Salute the captain = salute
Scrub the decks = pretend to scrub floor
Row ashore = sit in lifeboat and pretend to row
Overboard = fall out of lifeboat into sea
Swim ashore = swim on tummies or backs!
Land ahoy = look through telescope
Shark attack = shout help and get to any lifeboat as quickly as possible.

Helpful hint: Only introduce a few instructions at a time and practise, for example, just directions and lifeboats to start with. When they are familiar with the game, children could take turns to be the captain.

Get active!

Activity 3: Play with a rope

Why? A rope provides an imaginative focus to prompt children to practise their jumping, and moving on their tummies and backs.

Resources: A rope, with an adult at each end.

How? Line the children up comfortably along one side of the rope, with space to move.

- Adults lower the rope, or higher the rope, or make it wiggle according to the task
- Pretend it's a river; leap over it, do different jumps to get across, 'can you land on two feet? One foot? Can you jump from 2 feet to 2 feet? Can you run and leap across the river? Did you get wet?
- Pretend you are crocodiles and you are squirming along the river bed keeping your body under water, don't touch the rope!
- Have a tug of war!

Helpful hint: You can also use Lycra for a tug of war!

Safety issue: Leave the rope on the ground when jumping over, as jumping over a rope that is held high could lead to trips and falls.

Activity 4: Corners

Why? This versatile game can be organised to practise any locomotor skill.

Resources: A cone or marker in the centre of the room.

How? Organise a large group into 3-4 smaller groups, each go to an edge of the area, use corners if 4 groups.

- Give each group a name according to what you want to emphasise, for example, use colours, shapes or numbers
- Give each group an activity to do in turn, run, skip, jump, dance around the cone
- A variation is to give each group a name like 'the dancing group', 'the hopping group' and they move accordingly
- Children move round to a different corner and change their activity
- Focus on how you can get children to move on their tummies, like snakes or crocodiles to include tummy play
- Use some amusing actions like 'the silly walk' group, the walking backwards group and so on.

Helpful hint: Once children have got used to the game, they can decide on their own group identity, and others can guess it by the way they move, for example, animals. Adapt for smaller group with, for example 3 corners and 2 children.

Activity 5: Running games

Why? A fun way to get children active and out of breath! They practise their basic skills of running, stopping and dodging, jumping, hopping.

Resources: Cones or markers, bean bags, hoops.

How? Organise small groups of 3 or 4 children (more means they are less active and have to wait too long for a turn).

- Make a line of 3 cones or markers and put a hoop at the end, first child has bean bag
- Run in and out of the markers and drop a bean bag in the hoop:
  - either all children follow suit, each with own bean bag
  - or the next child runs in and out of the markers and brings the bean bag back and gives to next child
  - or run in and out of cones there and back and pass bean bag to next child
- There are many variations on this theme, using cones, hoops, bean bags in creative ways, for example, getting through a hoop or jumping into it during the run.

Helpful hint: Always ask yourself 'how active is this game?' and 'what skills are children practising?'.

Activity 6: Follow the leader

Why? This is an easy and fun way of getting children to practise their locomotor skills of jumping, hopping, etc.

Resources: Space!

How? Lead a crocodile of children around the space, doing different actions with your arms and legs. The funnier the better! You can do any movement skill. Move to the back of the line so children take turns to lead.

Helpful hint: Do things high and low, on tiptoes and creeping to challenge balance.

Activity 7: The bean game

Why? This is a fun game when children practise running, jumping, hopping and balancing skills.

Resources: Space!

How? Children move around quickly as 'runner beans' and stop and make a different 'bean' shape when instructed. The cues are:
Runner beans = running around
Broad beans = make a wide stretched shape
Jelly beans = wobbly bodies and wobbly walks
Chilli beans = explain these are hot! Hopping from one foot to the other
Beans on toast = curl into a small shape on the ground (later all run to centre of room and do this as if on one piece of toast!)
French beans: strike a pose and shout 'bonjour!'
Bean sprouts = stop and reach high on tip toes
Frozen beans = freeze in any shape
String beans = hold partners hand and run around
Beanstalk = pretend to climb.

Traffic lights - use red for stop, amber for get ready and walk around looking carefully, green for running.

Frogs and tadpoles – run when tadpoles and jump when frogs.

Animals – children travel around in different ways like animals, crab crawl (sideways with tummy facing up), bunny hop, horses gallop, caterpillar walk (all 4s), kangaroo.

Helpful hint: Easy start is to do running on the spot and only 2 different 'beans'.

Activity 8: The marching game

Why? Children practise controlling their movements in a fun, imaginative way.

Resources: A small space and music with a strong beat for marching.

How? Gather children in a circle, or a line, play good marching music, march normally, high knees, straight legs, slowly, double time, arms swinging, straight and bent, no arms, on tip toes, high, low, striding, tiny steps, on the outside of your feet.

Helpful hint: This is easy to do in a circle. Also children can take turns to lead. Ask children for different ideas for marching and follow their lead.

Activity 9: Bean bag play

Why? Using a bean bag to balance on different body parts challenges children to balance in different ways and on different body parts without realising.

Resources: A bean bag for each child.

How? Give children challenges, such as:
- Can you balance it on your foot, knee, shoulder, back, tummy, back of your hand?
- Can you flick it with your foot and catch it in your hand? Or flick it from your elbow to your hands?
- Can you toss the bean bag from hand to hand?

Helpful hint: Ask children to experiment with different places to balance the bean bag; can they move with the bean bag balanced on their body?

Get active!

Climbing and balancing skills (large equipment)

Climbing naturally involves the use of balancing skills. Developing skills is about increasing children's ability to climb and balance. This means that once they have conquered the climbing frame one way, they need a further challenge to tackle, for instance on steps with wider spaces, up a net or a pole, along a horizontal ladder. This way they test their own abilities, learn how to shift their weight from one part of their body to another in order to get safely to their goal. They practise the new challenge a number of times and this becomes easier, showing that their climbing skills have improved. In other words, it is only by testing your skill that you get better, for example, by skiing on a harder slope, or trying a more difficult maths problem.

An energising environment has a good range of large play equipment outdoors and where possible, indoors.

Climbing equipment should be available every day! Try to change the layout and adapt to make it more challenging.

Equipment

Large physical play equipment comes in many forms and each has its own benefits:

- Fixed, large multi-play pieces

- Fixed, low level trim trail pieces

- Portable, slot together equipment, with sections to add and change.

The type you choose depends on factors such as, the size and nature of your outdoor grounds and your indoor space, the age range of children, risk of vandalism, and budget.

You may choose a range of different types suitable for specific areas, such as a climbing wall and low level trim trail pieces.

The most important factors are to provide equipment that:

- Lends itself to a variety of levels and pathways so that children have to work out new approaches to climbing on, off, around, along, under and over

- Is flexible enough to meet the physical needs of children as they grow, and the age range in your nursery

- Children can arrange (some of) themselves to create their own challenges

- Children can climb, balance, hang from their arms, solve problems about how to use their bodies and do all these things with different levels of difficulty

- Has a suitable safety surface and robust risk assessments

- Is accessible for children with additional needs.

Consider how well your large equipment meets these points.

Activity: Using large equipment

Why? Climbing is a natural part of children's development and a fundamental movement skill. It not only develops every muscle in the body including strong hand muscles (for writing), but develops balance, and raises children's confidence enormously.

Resources: A range of challenging, adaptable large equipment.

How?
1. Portable climbing frames
- Arrange them differently throughout the week/month to create challenges
- Place platforms and the slide at different levels and angles
- Attach extra ladders and balancing beams.

2. Fixed climbing equipment
- Add portable equipment like boxes, steps, tunnels alongside the fixed equipment to add a new dimension, for example go down the slide straight through the tunnel!

3. Use small equipment alongside large equipment
- Hold a hoop for children to step or crawl through as they balance along a beam

- Ask them to balance a bean bag on their head as they walk along a bench.

4. Enable children to arrange some of the equipment themselves to create their own challenges

5. Know what children can do and what they should do next

6. Set challenging tasks using a problem-solving approach
- How can you reach the top without using your knees?
- How many different routes can you use to get to the top?
- Can you climb around the climbing frame rather than up and down?
- Can you walk across the beam sideways/backwards?
- Can you pull yourself along on your bottom/tummy?

Helpful hints: Adult presence and sensitive intervention in this area means children are more likely to take part for longer. Some children may choose not to climb because they are timid, or the equipment is dominated by a group of children, or it is boring or they are too busy doing other things.

Get active!

Ball skills (small equipment)

These skills involve throwing, catching, rolling, kicking, dribbling and striking a ball or other missile. They are difficult skills to learn and need lots of practise and direct teaching. These are often the most neglected skills in the early years because they are least planned for (Jo Blank, 2000). In order to develop these skills, you need to know the basic mechanics for example, throwing and catching.

An energising environment for developing ball skills has plenty of different sized balls of various weights, colours and textures, and soft throwing things like bean bags, with daily activities organised.

Throwing equipment should be available every day. You should provide:

- Light soft balls, the smaller the child the bigger and lighter the ball! Lighter balls travel more slowly through the air and are easier to catch. Covered balloons are a good idea for the youngest or smallest children

- Plenty of equipment so children can have a ball/bean bag each if in a small group activity

- Different sized balls for throwing with one hand and two hands

- Balls with bells in and/or with a textured covering are particularly good for children with sight impairment

- Targets to throw at (skittles, plastic bottles, chalk shapes) and to throw into (boxes, buckets, hoops, basketball rings)

- Markers for goal posts, to mark the area, to dribble balls around

- Bats and sticks, short-handled and big headed, to use with light medium-sized balls and balloons, short sticks to hit balls along the ground.

Activity 1: Helping children to throw overarm

Why? Throwing is a natural basic skill that is often neglected. Children need some clear guidance on how to throw. Having balls around is important for future games skills.

Resources: Bean bags, soft balls, and a target – a tree, bush, fence, a wall, something at eye level.

How? Work with one child or a group of 3 or 4.
Use a problem solving approach to improve the skill:
- 'What did you do to make the bean bag go high?'
- 'How can you throw the bean bag further?'
- 'What happens if you put one foot in front of the other and throw?'
- 'What about taking your arm right back to get ready?'
- 'Are you looking at the target?'

Know the mechanics!
- Stand sideways on
- Take your arm way back
- Opposite foot forward to throwing hand
- As you throw, weight transfers from back foot to front foot
- Follow through with throwing arm – long straight arm on release.

Helpful hint: Use soft balls and bean bags. Begin close and go further away as child gets better. Emphasise teaching one point at a time.

Activity 2: Throwing a big ball with 2 hands

Why? This is the easiest throw and can be done with very young children if using a light ball. It is a precursor to playing basketball and netball.

Resources: Large soft balls, a basketball hoop, or a person to catch!

How? Encourage the child to push the ball away from their body upwards to the target or forwards to you.

Know the mechanics!
- Step forward with left leg if right handed
- Hold the ball at the sides and towards the back
- Push the ball towards the target
- Arms follow through and are long at the end of the throw.

Helpful hint: Give one teaching point at a time.

Activity 3: Catching

Why? Catching is an essential basic skill that must be developed in the early years.

Resources: Use a big soft ball, progress to a large bouncy ball, and then a smaller ball.

What you do: Toss a large ball gently to the child who holds out their arms and 'traps' ball against chest. As they progress, they will watch the flight of the ball, and move their hands to make the catch. Bounce a ball and catch it.

Know the mechanics!
- Elbows are low; thumbs up or out
- Arms cushion the ball on contact and pull it towards the body.

Helpful hint: Use softly deflated balls, bean bags or soft toys to begin with; progress to balls of different size and weight.

Get active!

Activity 4: Rolling

Why? This is quite an easy basic skill to learn and success is easily achieved.

Resources: A large ball, or bean bags and a target like a cone, a box or a bucket upturned.

How?
- Demonstrate how to roll the ball towards the target, or have 3-4 children in a row and get them to roll the ball forwards to the next person through their legs
- 2 children can roll a ball to each other
- Roll the ball slowly, run after it to catch it
- Set up lots of targets, and use bean bags to slide along the floor to hit them
- Roll the ball or slide bean bag between 'goalposts'
- With younger children, sit down with legs apart, and roll the ball to each other.

Know the mechanics!
- Children will begin with feet together, but as they develop their skill they will stand with opposite foot forward
- Children will begin with hands either side of the ball, encourage them later to have one hand behind the ball
- Bend knees
- Eyes on target
- Take a back swing and then move weight forward as ball is released.

Helpful hint: Progress from large balls to smaller balls, rolling the ball from between the legs when children can stand up to roll.

Activity 5: Striking

Why? This is an important basic skill that is the foundation for many sports. It is a difficult skill to develop.

Resources: A large ball, short-handled, light-weight bats and light-weight balls, markers, cones.

How?
- Set up 2 cones and steer a big ball with your hand around the cones
- Do the same thing with a bat, pushing the ball along and controlling it
- Develop by hitting the ball through markers for a 'goal'.

Know the mechanics!
- Turn body sideways to push the ball forwards
- Use one hand
- Short sharp taps on the ball, and keep up with the ball
- Prepare to hit the ball by swinging the bat back behind you (take care!).

Helpful hint: Make the game harder by putting the cones closer and using a smaller ball.

Activity 6: Kicking and dribbling

Why? Kicking is an important ball skill for all children. It is a natural thing to do with feet and can be done with quite young children.

Resources: Markers for goals and for weaving in and out, a wall to kick at, large balls, sponge or 'not too bouncy' balls; use bean bags indoors.

How?
- Set up goals for children to kick at, or use a wall with or without a target. Set up markers to dribble ball around (and perhaps score goal at end)
- Use a problem solving approach to improve skill: 'what did you do to kick it so high?', 'can you kick it with both feet?'
- Can you use your feet to stop and trap the ball, encourage use of both hands and feet to do this.

Know the mechanics!
- Children will begin by standing and kicking
- they progress to running towards the ball and kicking it
- Prepare for a kick by taking leg back
- Children can kick with any part of foot as this is good preparation for future skills, practise with instep, outside of foot and front of foot
- Pass the ball from one foot to the other.

Helpful hint: Line up lots of balls for the same child, letting them kick each one in turn (perhaps at a target) without having to retrieve them. You may find that children already have a preferred foot.

Movement Skills and under 3s

For under 3s, it is about nurturing early movement patterns through natural movement play to help children develop their coordination and sense of balance, the basis for their future skills. By developing a good sense of proprioception children begin to work out how hard to throw a ball to reach a target. By stimulating the vestibular sense through spinning, rolling and turning upside they develop good balance, which will improve their ability to run and stop, and to jump and hop. Your role is to encourage children's natural movement, and prompt them to be active. They will take the lead and seek what their body needs, so the environment and resources are fundamentally important to inspire them. (See Section 1) For 2-3 year-olds, many of the activities in Section 2 can be simplified to enhance their experiences.

Activity 1: Bean bag toss

Why? This activity promotes the early development of ball skills and hand-eye coordination.

How? Toss the bean bags into the basket from a short distance. Sitting babies can do this too.

Helpful hint: Use soft toys or small boxes!

Get active!

Activity 2: Piling boxes

Why? It helps children develop manipulative and balance skills, encourages reaching and counting!

Resources: Lots of small boxes they can handle – cereal, mini cereal boxes etc.

How? Show how to pile them up and hand them one at a time to place on top. Enjoy knocking them down!

Helpful hint: Older toddlers may enjoy using different sized boxes

Activity 3: Walking the plank

Why? To develop balancing skills.

Resources: A piece of wood, about the same width as a bench.

How? Walk along the plank with arms out and jump off at the end into the 'sea'. Walk sideways and backwards along the plank, use a bean bag on the head, crawl along the plank forwards and backwards, with a bean bag on the back!

Helpful hint: Lift the plank at one end with books or blocks and see how that increases the challenge!

Activity 4: Reach and catch

Why? To encourage hand-eye coordination and manipulative skills.

Resources: Bubbles, scarves, feathers or balloons.

How? Blow bubbles for children to reach for or chase; use balloons to pat and reach for. Gently drift a scarf over the baby from their face down their body to their toes to encourage arm and leg movement and lots of giggles! Play peek-a-boo!

Helpful hint: Throw scarves or feathers in the air for babies to reach as they float down

Activity 5: Jumping the river

Why? Develops movement skills (jumping in different ways) and challenges them to jump as high/far as they can.

Resources: A rope, a chalk line or a piece of blue material.

How? Ask them to jump over the river as there are crocodiles! They can jump on 2 feet or leap from one foot to the other.

Helpful hint: They can also play splashing in the river and swimming on their tummies and backs!

Stepping stones: Play jumping across the river using hoops. Play jumping into the hoop and pretend they are splashing in a puddle. Jump into the hoop and out of the hoop, pretend they are speckled frogs and sing songs, put hands inside hoop and jump the feet in like a rabbit going down a hole.

Section 3: Movement and Dance

Why is it important?

Movement and dance explore 'where' and 'how' the body moves. This develops an awareness of space and improves the quality of movement. The 'where' and 'how' and with 'what' and with 'whom' the body moves are known as 'movement concepts', in other words, it is about 'movement understanding'.

Movement concepts (understanding) must be developed alongside **movement skills**.

As children improve their skills, they develop an understanding of where and how their body moves. They become aware of how much effort to use to throw a ball a long way; they learn how to avoid others as they run about.

The movement skill is what the body does. The movement concept is where, how, and with what or whom the skill is

performed. In order to use skills in different situations, (for example, climb a variety of equipment, run quickly or slowly to receive a ball) children need to be aware of:

Space – where the body moves, the space around them, directions, levels, their own personal space and general space.

Effort – how the body moves, how much effort they need to perform a skill, how hard to kick the ball to make it reach their partner, how slowly to move to balance across a beam.

Relationship – with whom or what the body moves, the relationship it has with objects and people, how to use the bat to hit the ball, how close to stand to the person who is throwing the ball.

How do children develop their movement concepts?

By practising skills children will naturally develop their movement concepts. So when helping children to throw, they will naturally work out how hard to throw it to reach the target. As skills develop, children will play with others; they can race each other, chase each other and play ball together. An awareness of others whilst on large play equipment can develop from a very early age. All this learning is developing their understanding of movement.

Movement and dance sessions are one of the most effective ways to develop children's awareness of where and how their bodies can move. Children learn how to move slowly, quickly, strongly, heavily and lightly. They learn to move forwards, backwards, high and low. They move alone, avoid bumping into others and do things with a partner and as a whole group. As children move in all these different ways, they build up their own movement vocabulary. They apply this knowledge when they express themselves imaginatively through movement, for example, pretending to be dinosaurs, or fireworks. They also draw on these skills when they face new physical challenges such as kicking a ball to a person, or weaving in and out of cones dribbling a ball. These new skills require control of speed and power (weight), ways of moving practised during movement and dance sessions.

When working with children, the best way to encourage them to improve the quality of what they do is to appeal to their imagination. For example, if you are 'going through the jungle' you can ask them to 'climb over branches, squirm under logs, and creep slowly through the trees so not to frighten the animals'. This will get them moving at different levels, at different speeds and with a gentle, light quality to their movements.

If you were pretending to be machines, movements could be fast or slow, jerky or smooth, heavy or light and with changes of direction.

This is the key to improving the quality of children's movement by developing tension in the muscles.

Development Matters gives importance to expressing feelings and ideas through movement:

- 'Uses movement to express feeling' 'creates movement in response to music' (30-50 months).
- 'Initiates new combinations of movement and gesture in order to express and respond to feelings, ideas and experiences' (40-60 months).
- 'Help children communicate through their bodies by encouraging expressive movement linked to their imaginative ideas' (40-60 months).

Reflection

Movement and dance is a major part of 'Expressive Arts and Design'; how do you include this in your curriculum planning? Which categories do your different activities fall into?
a) Directed movement or b) Expressive movement

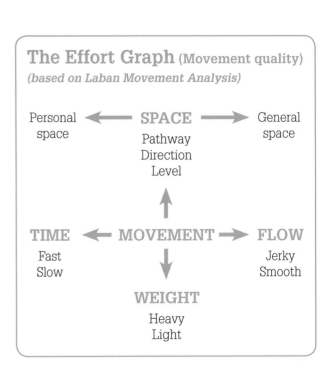

The Effort Graph (Movement quality)
(based on Laban Movement Analysis)

Personal space ← **SPACE** → General space

Pathway
Direction
Level

↑

TIME ← **MOVEMENT** → **FLOW**

Fast   Jerky
Slow   Smooth

↓

WEIGHT
Heavy
Light

The adult role

Leading movement and dance sessions

- Have plenty of enthusiasm and energy

- Believe in what you are doing, have confidence!

- Be involved, your movements are important so exaggerate everything

- Observe children's responses and be flexible and ready to change and move on; respond to their comments and mood and ask yourself, 'is it working?'

- Use powerful language, images and words to stimulate imagination

- Control your voice by using tone and expression sensitively to create atmosphere. For example, whisper slowly when creeping through the jungle, and be louder and talk faster when running away from lions.

Making it work

- Enlist extra help from staff where possible

- Begin with a calm quiet atmosphere; space children out, begin by doing simple loosening movements (see warm-up ideas in the next section)

- If this is new for you, begin by dancing with a small group for a few minutes

- Don't worry about the non-doers, let them watch, or give them an instrument to involve them. They will be absorbing more than you think!

- Aim for a quiet, organised ending, such as going to sleep, making themselves very small, tall, or stretching out or holding a position.

Get active!

Warm-up ideas

Why? To get children into the mood for a movement session with some easy, fun actions.

Resources: Enthusiasm and a fun approach! Know what you are going to do next so be prepared! Either use no music or music with a steady beat.

How?
Clapping and tapping
Clap slowly, clap high/low, clap in front/behind, to one side and the other, tap the knees and the floor (any combination!)

Steady beat activities
Tap the floor for 2 then knees for 2 then hands for 2 with or without music, or with words for 4 beats 'tap the floor, tap our knees, clap our hands and bend our knees!'

Action rhymes
I wiggle my fingers, I wiggle my toes, I wiggle my bottom and touch my toes
I stretch up tall, I bend down small, I turn around and touch the ground

I shake my hands, I shake my feet, I shake my body and march to the beat
Tip-toe, Tip-toe stand up very tall, tip-toe, tip-toe curl up very small
I touch my head, I touch my feet, I curl up small and go to sleep.

Handy tip: Choose one or two of the above, and repeat about 3 times

Development Matters gives importance to moving to rhythm:

■ 'Move their whole bodies to sounds they enjoy, such as music or a regular beat' (8-20 months).

Activity 1: Exercises to music

Why? This is a really enjoyable way of practising basic skills, learning about body parts, direction, levels, developing coordination and interpreting what you see into what your body does.

Resources: A lively piece of music you like with a good beat.

How? Develop a range of simple exercises using all the body parts. Consider all the limbs and joints and what they can do:

- **Legs** – bend, stretch, lift and kick in all directions, walk, skip, run in all directions
- **Arms** – lift, reach, circle in all directions, wave, stretch out to side, move out and in
- **Hands** – clap, wave, circle, twinkle, punch, click
- **Feet** – kick, tap, stamp, jump, stretch
- **Hips** – wiggle, circle, bend up and down
- **Shoulders** – lift and lower (together, separate), circle
- **Knees** and **elbows** – bend and stretch.

Choose simple moves and repeat the sequence, counting to 4 or 8. Choose 3 sequences and repeat these so the children get to know them.

Helpful hint: Begin with easy moves like wiggling hips, bending knees, add a clap or arm movement. Similarly, do easy walk forward, or 2 steps to side, add arm movement once they can repeat the first move.

Activity 2: Active 'Hello' song

Why? This is a fun enjoyable way to greet children at each session.

Resources: Enthusiasm!

How? Use your usual 'hello' song and put actions to it.

'Hello Hassan, hello Hassan, hello Hassan and how are you today?'
or
'Hello Evie, hello Evie, hello Evie, we're glad you're here today.'

Add a different action for each child as you sing; clap high in the air, rock from side to side, tap the feet on the floor with hands behind you, wave arms from side to side, sparkle with the fingers by stretching and curling them, roly poly arms down to your toes and back, stretch arms up high then out in front of you.

Helpful hint: When children are used to doing this activity sitting down, progress to standing and do more energetic actions.

Get active!

Activity 3: The body dance

Why? This is a great, fun way of helping children to understand how their bodies work.

Resources: Lively music with a good beat. Some visual aids, a heart shape, a long piece of red cord or elastic to represent blood.

How? See table opposite. Do each movement about 4-8 times each; when children have got used to the movements, ask them 'what do the lungs do?' (go in and out) 'what does the heart do?' (beats), 'what makes the muscles work?' (oxygen).

Helpful hint: Use slower music for younger children, talk with children beforehand about their hearts beating, and oxygen getting into their bodies. Don't worry about them completely understanding it, the fun movements are the most important!

Instruction	Action
Take in oxygen through the mouth	Open arms wide in different directions
Oxygen goes to lungs	Arms go in and out to side with bent elbows
The heart pumps the oxygen to the muscles	Straight arms open wide to the side and close with a clap while taking 4 steps to the side
Oxygen goes into the blood stream and goes all around the body	Walk/jog around the room wiggling the body
The oxygen reaches the muscles and makes them work	Stamp each foot 4 times, body builder arm actions, work shoulders, wiggle bottom and 'work' any other 'muscles' in the body
Begin the whole sequence again!	

Activity 4: Activities to music CDs

Why? This is an easy option for staff!! There is little preparation and organisation. There are many enjoyable activities and movement CDs available to purchase, such as Sticky Kids and Tumble Tots.

Warning: do not rely on these totally for children's movement experiences: their movement diet will become very limited, and with overuse, tedious.

Resources: Sticky Kids (Warm up! Work out! Bend and Stretch, Wiggle and Jiggle) – http://stickykids.net/

Tumble Tots (Tap and Boogie, Wiggle and Shake, Dance and Sing) – http://www.tumbletots.co.uk/

How you do it: Gather the children together in a circle and play the tape. Join in with the actions as the children will look to you for guidance. Be very clear with your movements and perform them well and with fun!

Handy tip: When children are familiar with the songs and movements, can you do it together without the music? Don't use all the tracks, select the favourites and ones that are most lively and fun. Let the children choose the tracks.

Ideas for expressive movement

Activity 1: Bubbles

Why? This is great for developing spatial awareness, thinking about different parts of the body, moving in different directions and moving very gently.

Resources: A sense of fun and excitement, an expressive voice and a good imagination!

How? Pretend to blow bubbles and tell children that one has landed on each of them. They are now inside a huge bubble!

- First of all they gently feel all around them with their hands, how big the bubble is and where it starts
- They then explore the bubble with their feet, their elbows, their head and any other body parts, being very careful not to pop it (if anyone does pop it just blow them another!)
- Then they stand up very slowly and start to take their bubble for a walk, being careful not to get close to anyone else. They can walk forwards, backwards and sideways; they could crawl along slowly
- A great finish to the session is for everyone to make a loud POP! And do a huge jump!

Helpful hint: Encourage them to move in different directions rather than round in a circle following each other. Encourage different types of movement such as creeping, walking on tiptoes, crawling, stretching out their arms and legs.

Activity 2: Puppets

Why? This is a fun way to learn how different parts of our bodies can move, to develop rhythm, and body vocabulary.

Resources: A real puppet with strings, the story of Pinocchio. You may or may not choose to use music, if so 'The Sting Theme' (The Entertainer by Scott Joplin) works well.

How? Explain that they are puppets with string attached to all the different parts of their body. Have a string puppet to show them, or use the story of Pinocchio.

Begin with them lifting their knees up with the string attached to their hands, then, suggest they lift their toes, their elbows, hands, head, shoulders etc. You can also be the puppeteer and pull the string for them to move specific body parts.

Older children can join a partner, one is the puppeteer and one is the puppet.

Activity 3: Machines

Why? This is a good activity to practise moving in different directions, strongly and directly, and fast and slow. It is great for using and becoming aware of specific body parts, for remembering simple sequences through repetition and developing a good sense of rhythm.

Resources: An option is to use music with a strong beat. Use books with machines, robots, a factory. Follow up a visit to a garage or building site.

How? Ask children what machines they know – washing machine, tumble drier, sand wheel, water pump, car engines, conveyer belt in supermarket, drinks machines, diggers.

Ask them to move like a machine part, and use their ideas. Suggest some simple moves:

- **Whole body** – bob up and down, stretching arms as you come up
- **Arms** – turn one arm or both arms around in a circle like a wheel turning, punch fists up in the air alternately 4 times, then out in front 4 times, stretch arms out then draw in 4 times, circle both arms around in front like a washing machine
- **Legs** – kick out feet alternately 4 times, bend knees low and stretch up high, lift knees alternately 4 times.

Once children can repeat the move say 5 times, add a change of direction or a change of speed, for example, bob up and down then do a quarter turn, repeat; do 2 fast arms to side and 2 slow ones; do 2 fast arm circles and 2 slow ones as if the washer is slowing down.

Older children Choose 3 different moves, split the children into 3 groups, give each group one move, or let them choose their own. One group begins then the next starts then the next until they are like one big machine working. If they can remember all 3 moves, and perform them in a sequence, let one group begins, then the other group begins when the first group moves onto the second move. Be very clear about how many times they repeat the same move. This is a very effective group dance!

Helpful hint: Make sure you choose moves based on what the children do so they can make sense of the machines theme. Liken their moves to machines they know about. Ask them to perform their moves very clearly; are their hands flat with fingers stretched or do they make a fist? Are they moving fast or slow? Are they reaching high or down low? Are their movements jerky or smooth?

Get active!

Activity 4: In the jungle

Why? This is an exciting way to explore all the movements in the Effort Graph on page 30. It is great for creating an imaginative story.

Resources: Ideas about the jungle and jungle stories. You may like to use a rope or piece of blue material for a river.

How? Begin to build a story; pretend you are in the jungle and you have to creep very slowly so you do not disturb the animals (ask them which animals are in the jungle). You have to squirm under and climb over branches. You take a windy pathway, and look behind you as you tread carefully. You stop and look around and listen, what can you hear?

Take ideas from the children and go along with them, for example, you suddenly hear a swishing noise, what do you do? Run away quickly? Stand still very quietly? Hide behind a tree? Ask them 'what shall we do?'
You come to a river, how will you get across? Stepping stones? Swing on a rope? Swim? Jump? It may not be deep so you can wade across. Everyone can try the different ideas. You could have a rope or a piece of blue material for the river. There may be crocodiles in the river!

Ask them to pretend to be the animals in the jungle, monkeys, snakes, elephants, tigers. They could be with a friend who falls and hurts themselves. They have to go and fetch help.

Helpful hint: You could begin by packing your rucksack – what do they need to take into the jungle? Let the story develop with the help of the children, go with the flow. Make sure you include moving high, medium and low, creeping slowly, running fast, zigzagging, moving in different directions.

Activity 5: Under the sea

Why? This is a fun way to explore a range of movements using imagination. It can link with stories and their knowledge of the seaside.

Resources: Clear movements, an interesting voice and enthusiasm! Link with a story, for example, *The Rainbow Fish* by Marcus Pfister, *Tiddler* by Julia Donaldson. Also provide other activities such as water play with different sea creature toys. If you would like to use music, 'Octopus's Garden' by the Beatles is a good one, focus on moving like an Octopus!

How? Ask them what lives under the sea and how it moves, fish, whales, sharks, octopus, swordfish, turtles, starfish, lobster, crabs, seals, dolphins and so on.

Practice moving like the different fish and underwater creatures. Ask them to choose a creature, move like it and for others guess what it is.

Encourage them to:

- Move on their tummies, as well as their feet
- Move with their backs to the ground and on hands and feet, moving sideways like a crab
- Use their whole bodies to show how a dolphin moves
- Think about their body shape for a star fish and a swordfish
- Show how some fish are light and fast and other creatures are slow and heavy.

Helpful hint: As a follow-up session, you can split the children into groups of different types of fish, one group moves and stops and hovers, then another group starts, moving in and out and around each other. This will encourage working as a group, pathways, and being aware of others in space. Emphasise how fast or slowly each group moves.

Development Matters gives importance to how adults:

- 'Encourage body tension, such as stretching, reaching, curling, twisting and turning' (22-36 months).

Development Matters gives importance to providing movement sessions linked to experiences:

- 'Lead imaginative movement sessions based on children's current interests, such as space travel, zoo animals or shadows' (30-50 months).

Ideas for expressive movement

Activity 6: At the park

Why? This draws on their real experiences, they can all imagine being on the slides and roundabouts. It explores a range of movement skills and qualities. Safety aspects can easily be brought in.

Resources: Your enthusiasm and your own body movements that should be larger than life and easy to understand and copy.

How? Pretend you are going to the park with your friend and a parent. Begin by holding hands to cross the road to go to the park. Look both ways before you cross.

When safely in the park, you run to your favourite piece of equipment (ask them what it is). Then try the slide, roundabouts, seesaw etc and ask them to pretend to do the movements. They could hold hands in a small group to be on a roundabout. Remember to climb the steps to the slide, reach high on the climbing frame.

Helpful hint: Think of changes of speed, slow up the steps, fast down the slide, roundabouts go slow then speed up.

Activity 7: Free movement to music

Why? Children listen and move naturally to the beat of the music. They will interpret the mood and move accordingly. This is truly self-expression.

Resources: A music player children can use themselves, a range of music from around the world, to provide different moods, beats and sounds. ARC World music is a good source. Provide scarves, instruments and streamers for children to dance with. Set aside a space for dancing.

How? Enable children to play music and dance freely in an area of the nursery. Have this available daily. An adult can model dancing to the music to introduce this idea to children.

Helpful hint: When you dance with children, mirror some of the movements they do. This gives importance to what they do and can prompt further ideas. Model moving high, medium and low, to widen their scope of movement. You can also talk to the children about the music, how does it make them feel? How does it make them want to move?

Activity 8: Bonfire and fireworks dance

Why? Many children will experience Bonfire night and be able to draw on their experiences to interpret into exciting movements. It explores the extremes of sudden, explosive jumping (fireworks) and soft gentle swirling movements (smoke).

Resources: You may like to introduce percussion to represent the different types of fireworks, or the changing nature of the fire.

How? Talk with children about what they have seen and heard, the bonfire, Guy Fawkes, fireworks. Develop language such as 'swirling smoke', 'leaping flames', 'sudden bangs', 'bright, sparkly stars'. Talk about the sounds, whoosh! Shhhhhhh...! bang! Ssssss! And try and make them!

Decide together which percussion instruments to use for different fireworks, cymbals, tambourine, bells etc. Fireworks: Ask them to show you how a rocket takes off and what it does in the sky. They can add the sound effects for fun too!

Mimic the movements of different fireworks, such as Catherine wheels, rockets, snow storms, sparklers.

Emphasise the changes in speed as the wheel gets faster and faster and explore the vestibular senses! They can twirl on their feet, bottom, or move their arms to show the wheel.

Use their fingers, toes and whole bodies to show twinkly sparks. Emphasise sudden jerky movements. Encourage them to land safely by bending their knees.

Bonfire: Pretend to build the bonfire as a group, carrying heavy wood, do this in 2s. Change this into being the bonfire, so in small groups they make a group shape, with bits of wood sticking out.

Change this into being the fire when it is lit, so they swirl like the smoke, they are small flames that gradually become large flames leaping into the sky.

Helpful hint: Emphasise the quality of their movements, like stretching fingers and toes, softly floating their hands around their bodies for smoke. For older children, in a second/third session you could develop a whole dance, beginning with the bonfire building, the fire growing and then the fireworks to finish.

Get active!

Activity 9: Superheroes!

Why? This is a popular theme for all children. It hooks right in to their interests and explores a range of both strong and powerful movements, and more fluid, softer movements. It gives positive value to superhero play, which is a very important part of many children's lives.

Resources: Enthusiasm! A general knowledge of popular superheroes, how they move, and their special powers.

How? Ask children how the superhero moves. Take different ideas, with some fast and some slow moves. Build on this, encouraging them, for example, to spread out their fingers as they climb the wall, placing their hands very carefully, and making their movements very smooth and flexible. Take a run and leap high into the sky! Improve the quality of their movements, by using the effort graph, thinking about, fast, slow, light and heavy, and all the spatial areas.

Explore the way the superhero fights, or moves with kicks, or karate moves, making sure they have plenty of space around them! Try these moves in slow motion, and emphasise the hands, feet, stance, and levels; help them to really think about the movement with their whole body.

Explore the superhero's magic powers. This could be Xray vision, turning into a machine, or developing super strength. Get children to think about what happens before this power is used, to really imagine the details.

With older children, ask them to make up their own superhero. How do they move, if they fight how do they do this? What are their super powers? You could demonstrate by suggesting one, for example, who twirls around and falls to the ground to become invisible, or has a magic wand that creates stars. If this is developed over a few sessions, you could create a small group dance, for example, all striding slowly towards each other doing karate hands, then twirling around and disappearing, then appearing somewhere else as a normal person!

Helpful hint: The best source of ideas is the children as they will know far more about this area! Make sure you draw on their ideas. They can make up stories, draw and paint, and adults can record and help them make their own books. This theme provides so much rich and imaginative learning!

Activity 10: The weather dance

Why? Children can easily draw on their experiences of the weather to prompt their movements. It gives children plenty of opportunities to move in different ways exploring the range of effort qualities.

Resources: Percussion instruments, bells, you choose!

How? Talk to children about the different weather and decide together what percussion best suits for example, rain, sunshine, rumbling clouds, storm, thunder and lightning.

Begin to play each instrument to represent each type of weather and prompt them to move like the raindrops, to move faster as it changes from a few spots to a heavy downpour. Develop this into playing in puddles, splashing and jumping over them.

Explore other weather movements, sunshine movements, stretching out slowly then going behind a cloud, thunder with rolling heavy body movements, lightening with sudden jumps and limbs that shoot out.

Build this into a dance sequence by leading with the percussion and children responding accordingly to the recognisable sounds.

Helpful hint: Let the children also use the percussion, or they could dance in pairs or small groups of 3, one playing percussion and the others moving.

Movement and dance for under 3s

Babies and toddlers respond to music naturally with their bodies and love action songs. These should be a large part of everyday activities, both planned and spontaneous. Singing and dancing are essential foundations for language, physical development and PSED.

Babies and toddlers need a rich music and movement environment:

■ Learn rhymes and songs by heart so that you can sing regularly with children and introduce new ones to them

■ Don't have general background music in your room, this will desensitise children and yourselves to sounds and music

■ Plan a regular rhyme time, which includes lots of action songs

■ Play different types of music from around the world with lively and calm beats and dance with the children;

have scarves and streamers available for toddlers indoors and outdoors

■ Bounce babies on your knee singing songs and clapping hands

■ When children are playing, sing songs that go with their play, such as 'The Wheels on the Bus' or 'Incy Wincy Spider', 'Old McDonald had a Farm' to help them make connections.

There are numerous sources for action rhymes and songs, including traditional nursery rhymes. The EYFS gives excellent guidance for encouraging babies and toddlers to respond to music and rhythm.

2-3s

As well as enjoying action rhymes and dancing to music, this age group will enjoy joining in some of the more simple dance and movement ideas for 3-5s in this section.

Section 4: Movement and the Curriculum

Why is it important?

This section explores how children will learn best by having the options to approach all areas of learning in a physical way.

PSED: Physical activities develop children's self-esteem and confidence, as they feel pride in their physical achievements and develop their body awareness, they gain a sense of who they are. Physical activities help children to understand rules, enjoy doing things together, make friends and help each other. Children can manage their strong feelings through movement. Frustration and anger can be controlled through guided physical actions and joy expressed and prompted through running and dancing. Children can feel empathy to each other if they are hurt through tumbling.

Communication and Language: Movement activities are often social activities and so they naturally lend themselves to talking. Movement is also a language of the body.

Literacy: Books and stories are a rich source of physical drama! Bring stories to life through movement.

Mathematics: Physical activities are an excellent, natural and meaningful way to learn about numbers and shapes, mathematical language, and solving problems.

Understanding the World: Expressive movement is an ideal medium for helping children to understand so much about their world. For example, they can learn about under the sea, machines, different feelings, animals and insects.

Expressive Arts and Design: Going big in art is a great physical way to be expressive, and adventurous role play can fuel the imagination. Movement and dancing are fundamental to this area of learning.

The adult role

The adult has a crucial role in enabling children to learn in the most effective way. The EYFS introduces three key 'Characteristics of Effective Learning', which are strongly rooted in fundamental early years research and philosophy.

'In planning and guiding children's activities, practitioners must reflect on the different ways that children learn and reflect these in their practice' Statutory Framework for the Early Years Foundation Stage 1.10

Characteristic of Effective Learning	Physical link
Playing and exploring: This is about children being engaged in what they are doing by exploring and finding things out. They initiate activities, are willing to have a go, take a risk and learn by trial and error.	Babies and young children have a natural urge to find out what their bodies can do through free movement and fun, challenging activities.
Active learning: This is about children being motivated through being involved, and concentrating on what they do. They keep on trying, and enjoy achieving what they set out to do.	Babies and young children are naturally driven to move their bodies in ways that help them develop. They practise skills over and over until they are mastered, and are proud of their success.
Creating and thinking critically: This is about children thinking. They have their own ideas, make links, and choose their own ways to do things.	Babies and young children find their own best ways of moving. They make natural links to learning as they travel under, over and through climbing equipment; they create and adapt their own physical challenges given the right environment and equipment.

Get active!

A movement approach to Personal, Social and Emotional Development

Physical success gives children a sense of pride and achievement as they find out what their bodies can do. As children develop their body awareness they become aware of who they are. Physical activities are often social; children have fun running together, chasing, riding bikes, jumping, building and dancing. This naturally helps them to understand rules, enjoy doing things together, make friends and help each other. Children can manage their strong feelings through movement. Frustration and anger can be controlled through guided physical actions and joy expressed and prompted through running and dancing. Children share space on physical equipment and learn to be considerate, and wait turns; they feel empathy to each other if they are hurt.

Movement Play

When children move freely they feel at home in their bodies. They become aware of themselves and who they are. This is important from birth to 5 years and beyond. When children have strong feelings of anger, frustration, confusion, and also joy, delight and excitement, they learn to manage these emotions more easily through being physical.

Movement Skills

The activitiy games in Section 2 and in this section under Mathematics, will help children to understand rules, be social, and enjoy the 'feel good' factor of group activities. As they master a new skill and develop physical competence, they grow in confidence and self assurance.

Movement and Dance

Children express how they feel through how they move. They interpret ideas in their own way, exploring feelings and life experiences. Different types of music can invoke a range of feelings and encourage spontaneous expression.

Get active!

A movement approach to Communication and Language

Learn about body language using music (2-5s)

Why? It develops children's communication skills by helping them to read emotions through non-verbal signals.

Resources: A range of music that prompts different moods, like sadness, joy, anger, pride. Classical music often has this variety of moods, and music from around the world.

How? Play the music and ask children how it makes them feel. How do they move when they feel like this? For example:

- **Sad** – slow movements, dragging the feet, head down, body is slumped
- **Happy** – jumping around, big, bouncy movements, open arms, explosive and upward focus
- **Angry, cross** – strong movements, clenched fists, stern face, stamping, downward focus.

Helpful hint: Ask children to notice how each other move, and to describe it. Describe the movement you see everyday. 'I can see that you are cross because you are stamping your feet/ kicking the box'. Encourage children to talk to each other as they play, for example, 'excuse me', 'how many skittles did you knock down?', 'it's your turn first then mine'.

Under 2s: Lively music – bounce babies and toddlers on your knee and dance around with them in your arms. Toddlers will enjoy jigging about. Calm music – rock babies and toddlers in your arms and on your knee. Help them feel the different moods of the music.

Give words to children's movements (0-5s)

Why? This helps them to understand vocabulary and make sense of their world. It values their movement.

How? Describe what they are doing, for example, you are spinning round really fast! You are balancing on one hand and stretching out your legs! You are rolling on the floor with your arms tucked into your chest! You are crawling really fast!

Helpful hint: As they become used to the language of movement, ask them to explain their movements, and describe what other children do, for example, 'How did you manage to get inside that box?', 'What did you do to balance across the plank sideways?', 'How are you going to get down?'

Use clear and expressive vocabulary when leading rhyme and movement sessions (2-5s)

Why? This expands children's vocabulary and makes new words meaningful.

How? Think of words that express movement and an imaginative picture, for example, swirl and whirl round and round like the smoke, squirm and slither along the floor like a snake, quiver and shiver like a jellyfish! Wibble wobble like a jelly.

Helpful hint: Always show what you mean with your body. With younger children, and those with EAL, use simpler language as you say the words that describe actions clearly.

Under 2s: As babies crawl, roll, pull themselves up, give words to their actions. As toddlers run, roll over, spin around repeat words, make them rhyme, and match their movements to nursery rhymes; for example, spinning, spinning round and round, Teddy Bear, Teddy Bear turn around, Roly Poly ever so slowly, up and down up and down, Jack and Jill went up the hill, tall like a house, small like a mouse, aeroplanes aeroplanes all in a row, aeroplanes aeroplanes ready to go, aeroplanes aeroplanes up in the sky, aeroplanes aeroplanes ever so high! Aeroplanes aeroplanes coming to land, aeroplanes aeroplanes down on the ground. Zoom zoom zoom we're going to the moon, Zoom zoom zoom we'll get there very soon, 5, 4, 3, 2, 1, Blast off!

Get active!

Telling stories through movement (2-5s)

Why? By acting out stories, children will remember them, understand the story better, know about the beginning, middle and end, understand the sequence of the story, the characters and the language. They will recall their knowledge of the story and be able to reflect on, adapt and explore their ideas and own understanding.

Resources: Books with a 'movement' element, see list below.

How? Make sure the children are familiar with the story before they begin to represent it through movement.

Know the story well yourself so that you can develop the key movement aspects. Practise telling it without the book.

Work out the type of movements that will represent the story best, for example, how the different fish move in the *Rainbow Fish* by Marcus Pfister, how the dinosaurs move, and other animals in *The Animal Bop* by Jan Ormerod.

Think how you might best describe these movements, using the effort graph. For example, small fish may 'dart', change direction quickly, are light and quick. Lions may 'prowl', moving slowly, smoothly and heavily through the jungle. Snakes 'squirm and wiggle', are slow and fast

Handy tip: You can choose to use elements of the story , for example, the animal movements, or follow the whole story, or both.

You can practise and develop some aspects of the story before you go through the main story, for example the fish, giant or animal movements. This may be enough for the first session.

Under 2s: When sharing books, emphasise the sounds and actions in the story, make it physical for the child, for example, use your hands to creep up their legs and arms for Incy Wincy spider, and tickle them for Hickory Dickory Dock, let them fall gently through your legs for Humpty Dumpty, move their legs up and down for the Grand Old Duke of York, hide under some material just like Spot hides.

IDEA! A listening run! – children run for 10 or 20 paces instead of walking between stopping places, where they stand and listen for different sounds!

Telling traditional Fairy Stories through movement (2-5s)

Resources: Traditional stories like Little Red Riding Hood, Jack and the Beanstalk, Three Little Pigs, The Billy Goats Gruff.

How? Make sure the children are familiar with the story, and you can tell it without the book. Explore the movement elements within the story. How does Red Riding Hood move? She might skip happily through the forest. How do the trees move? They are very tall and move slowly in the breeze. How does the fox move? Slyly and slowly creeping through the forest.

Ask the children to become the various characters and natural features. For example, the trees in the wood, the river flowing fast under the bridge, the beanstalk winding up to the sky.

Helpful hint: Ask questions to provoke imagination and prediction...What might happen if...Red Riding Hood wandered off the path? The wolf was a friendly wolf? It was raining? What might happen if...Jack had 10 magic beans? No one bought the cow? Jack fell down the beanstalk?

Books for telling stories through movement (there are lots more!)

Lost in the Snow by Ian Beck
Small Bear Lost by Martin Wadell
Mr Wolf's Week by Colin Hawkins
Beautiful Bananas by Elizabeth Laird, Liz Pichon
The Dance of the Dinosaurs by Colin and Jacqui Hawkins
Bumpus Jumpus Dinosaurumpus by Tony Mitton and Guy Parker-Rees
Where's the Gold? by Pamela Allen
Doing the Animal Bop by Jan Ormerod and Lindsey Gardiner
Follow my Leader by Simon Puttock and Philip Hopman
We're Going on a Bear Hunt by Michael Rosen and Helen Oxenbury
We're Going on a Lion Hunt by David Axell
Walking through the Jungle by Julie Latcome
Rainbow Fish and the Sea Monster's Cave by Marcus Pfister
Whoosh around the Mulberry Bush by Jan Ormerod and Lindsey Gardiner
If You're Happy and you Know it! by Jan Ormerod and Lindsey Gardiner
Little Red by Lynn Roberts
Stick Man by Julia Donaldson and Alex Scheffler

Get active!

A movement approach to Literacy: Writing

Games with instruments (2-5s)

Why? This helps children to listen carefully and to distinguish between different sounds.

How?
Hide and seek: Hide musical instruments around the garden. Children play them when they find them and everyone runs to where they hear it playing!

Move to the beat: Play a range of instruments loudly, softly, quickly and slowly and ask children to take small, large, light or heavy steps according to the sound.

Helpful hint: Let the children play the instruments, once they are used for the game.

Under 2s: Play instruments loudly and softly with children and talk about whether they are 'loud', 'soft' or 'quiet'. Talk about how drums go 'bang bang', triangles and bells go 'ting ting', cymbals go 'crash'.

Learning letters through movement: Initial letter sounds (2-5s)

Why? This is a fun, active way to learn and consolidate letter sounds.

How? Use actions to represent the initial letter sounds, j – jjj...jump, h – hhh...hop, c – ccc...crawl, l – lll..leap, t – ttt...tiptoe, m – mmm...march, b – bbb...bounce, s – sss...slide etc.

With older children: develop this by connecting their name to an action, for example, Jo jumps for joy! Simon slides on a sausage! Lola leaps over a lion!

Helpful hint: Make sure you pronounce the letters correctly, how they sound in the word.

Learning syllables through movement: Rhythmic names

Why? This is a fun, meaningful activity that combines movement with understanding syllables.

Resources: Enthusiasm!

How? In a circle, begin with your name and do movements that match the rhythm of the name 'No..ah' Sam..an..tha', Fre...ddy', Am..ir..a'. You may do a jump and a stretch for 2 syllables, or a kick, a stamp and a turn for 3 syllables. Ask the children to do the same for their own name, suggest some moves. Everyone tries the moves each child has created.

Helpful hint: Try clapping the syllable first to give them an idea of rhythm.

Learning letters through movement: Letter shapes (3-5s)

Why? Children can 'feel' the letter shapes as they physically create them. It is a fun and effective way to strengthen their knowledge and understanding.

Resources: Nothing except your body! Or you can use streamers, scarves or ribbons.

How? Ask the children to make the letter shapes with their bodies. Use the letters they are familiar with, like

those in their names or from stories. They can also work in pairs to make a 'j' or a 'b' for example. Use fingers or streamers to 'write' giant letters in the air. Walk/run/jump/hop around the letter shape on the ground.

Helpful hint: Ask children to make their own letter shape and others to guess what it is.

Under 3s: Use streamers, scarves and ribbons to wave around in time with music to strengthen arms and make visual patterns.

Get active!

A movement approach to Mathematics

Activity 1: Skittles – counting, adding and taking away

Why? Playing skittles is an ideal time to count, add on and take away.

Resources: Skittles and balls, bean bags indoors.

How? Ask children to count:
- How many are there altogether?
- How many have they knocked down?
- How many are left standing up?

Helpful hint: Use a bigger ball for younger children for more immediate success. They can roll it with 2 hands. Don't forget the mechanics! (See Section 2, Activity 4: Rolling). Make your own skittles with plastic bottles or large washing liquid containers filled with sand.

Activity 2: Locomotor games – counting (2-5s)

Why? This is a fun way to include counting naturally in active games.

Resources: Hoops, bean bags, cones.

How? Set up a small active team game where children can practise their locomotor skills. Choose 3 things, for example, jump 5 times in the hoop, run to the cone, and throw a bean bag in the bucket, run back to the start. There are numerous possibilities! Children will develop their own circuits when they are familiar with the process.

Under 2s: All these games can be simplified for younger children who can walk. Just remember 1,2,3,...Go! Jump! Throw!

Activity 3: Target throwing – counting

Why? It is natural for children to count as they practise their target throwing.

Resources: Containers on the ground for throwing into, such as buckets, hoops, boxes. Big targets to throw at, fixed onto a wall or fence, such as a hoop, big circlular face with a hole for a mouth, numbers or shapes painted onto the wall/fence. Bean bags, quoits, small balls or arrow toys to throw with one hand. Inside you could use small soft toys!

How? Have a marker where children stand to throw. Attach a target to a wall/fence to throw at (same height as them) Or, place a container on the ground so they toss the ball or bean bag into it. (Be clear about the skills you want to develop).

Ask them: How many bean bags/ balls can you get into the hoop/bucket? If we all got one ball in, how many is that altogether? Can you hit the number 10, 20, 50 on the target?

Helpful hint: It is easier to toss things into a container than throw at a higher target. (See Section 2, Activity 1). Begin nearer, then move further away to make it harder. Overarm throwing is an advanced skill so do this with older children. Have clipboards handy to mark scores.

Under 2s: Skittles, targets and running – counting

Why? Children will play with balls from a very early age. They will love knocking things down! Simple counting goes naturally with these games.

Resources: As above, only bigger and lighter balls/bean bags, 'closer' targets, cones.

How? Set up containers to toss balls/bean bags into. Set up skittles or bottles to knock down. Get children to roll the ball to the skittles or toss it into the container. Say 1.2.3...go! Emphasise the counting. Count the skittles as you pick them up, just have 2-5 skittles. Count to 10 as children run around a cone.

Helpful hint: Let the parents know the games the children have been playing and how they have learned to count and add on one more. Let them know what the children have enjoyed doing and encourage parents to do this at home.

Get active!

A movement approach to Mathematics

Activity 4: Ordering numbers

Why? This helps children to be familiar with sequencing numbers, putting them in the right order.

Resources: Number cards on string to place around children's necks like a necklace.

How? Ask the children to stand in the right order: 1-5 or 1-10, ask them to do it as quickly as they can.
Take 2 children out, then ask them to find their place again. Ask 2 numbers to run and change places, see who gets there first.

Helpful hint: To extend this for older children, you can add and subtract with some children, for example, 2 add 1 equals 3. Stand in 2s and see what number you make, 24, 37.

IDEA! Make a number track using dinosaur footsteps, stepping stones, footprints and children follow these, searching for the next one! Treasure at the end!

Activity 5: Under, over, down and through climbing equipment – mathematical language and counting (0-5s)

Why? Scrambling around climbing equipment is the best time to use mathematical language because it is such a body felt and visual learning experience.

Resources: A range of physical play equipment, including planks, tunnels, steps and ladders, slide.

How? As you observe and help children on the climbing equipment, talk about where they are moving, for example, through the tunnel, under the plank, over the top, down the slide.

Helpful hint: Counting – make a circuit and number the sections so that children follow the numbers as they go along.

Activity 6: Active counting rhymes!

Why? This can be more fun and meaningful if the children physically take part in the rhyme with their whole body. When children see numbers represented by people, they can clearly see for example, what 2, 3 and 4 means.

How?
5 Currant Buns – children are the buns, one child buys the bun and takes a child's hand to lead them away.

5 Green Speckled Frogs – 5 children are frogs on logs and jump into the pool.

5 Little Monkeys – 5 children jump up and down, fall off the bed etc.

10 Green Bottles – 10 children are bottles and fall off the wall.

5 Little Ducks – 5 children swim across the pond, mother duck quacks and they join her one by one. Children swim on tummies and backs on the floor.

Helpful hint: Always ask older children to count how many are left.

Under 2s: Bounce babies up and down on your knee and do the actions in a **big** whole body way. Toddlers will get used to hearing numbers.

Get active!

A movement approach to Mathematics

Activity 7: Parachute games

Recognise numbers, add and subtract

Why we do it: This is a fun way to do lots of maths thinking! You can make it as easy or difficult as you like.

Resources: Parachute and number cards on string as necklaces for children or sticky number labels.

How? Give lots of number-based instuctions, depending on children's level of understanding, such as:

- Numbers 3 and 5 change places
- Run around the outside if you are less than 7
- Run into the middle if you are more than 5.

Helpful hint: Make sure the 'number necklaces' are safe to wear and run around in.

Parachute counting game

Resources: A parachute, different things that are easy to pick up. Put them all underneath the parachute.

How? Ask specific children to run in and collect 3 green balls, 2 things that are round, 4 bean bags, etc. Choose the action to suit the child's understanding.

Use balls to bounce up and down on the parachute and count how many bounces before they bounce off!

Helpful hint: Continue the game by reversing the instructions to take things back underneath.

For younger children: use colour, ask children with blue shoes, wearing something red, to run into the middle and back or run across to the other side of the parachute.

IDEA! Don't forget the games 'What time is it Mr Wolf' 'Grandmother's footsteps' 'Hide and seek' are all good counting games!!

Activity 8: Garden treasure hunt – counting, sorting, comparing

Why? Children enjoy finding natural materials and counting at the same time.

Resources: Cards with a list of numbers and the items to find: 1 feather, 2 pine cones, 3 twigs, 4 leaves, 5 stones Adapt according to the time of year and what is in your garden. Also give each child a bag. You can also collect elsewhere and scatter them around your area.

How? Stick an example of the item onto the card. Ask the children to find the things around the garden, they can work in 2s or in teams with an adult and see who can find everything the fastest!

When they return, they empty their bags and sort everything out, counting again.

Talk about the different sizes of the stones and twigs Who has the biggest/heaviest/longest/shortest twig/ stone etc.

Helpful hint: Also talk about where they found things, where the feathers may have come from, what trees the leaves came from etc. (Communication and Language and Understanding the World).

Under 2s: Ask younger children to find 1,2, or 3 things and do this together. With babies, let them touch the leaves on the trees, handle stones, feel the grass and crawl on it.

IDEA! Measure a large area – how many strides? How many footsteps? How long does it take to run around it?

Get active!

A movement approach to Mathematics

Activity 9: A number or shape hunt – counting, recognising numbers and shapes

Why? This is an exciting way to recognise numbers or shapes and to count!

Resources: Photos of the places where the numbers/ shapes are to be found. In these places you have left a card with instructions, for example, 5 jumps, stand on one leg and count to 10, run to the tree and back.

How? Give children the numbered/shapes cards with photos on. They go to the place on the photo and match the number or shape. They perform the task written on the card. This can be done with one child or a small group.

Helpful hint: When children are used to the game, let them help prepare the clues. Give them a clip board to tick off the numbers or shapes they find.

Under 2s: Hide a group of the same things in the sand or underneath material, anywhere around their play areas (plastic animals, shells, pine cones). Take them on a walk around their areas and collect the group of things you have hidden. Count them altogether when you have finished.

IDEA! Remember to talk to them about capacity in sand and water play! It is all about space and measure! Full, half-full, empty, how many cups to fill the jug? Check you have good equipment for filling and emptying.

Activity 10: Large-scale construction – space, shape and measure (2-5s)

Why? This is a very physical construction activity, and children naturally think about space and shape as they solve problems to build. It is a great social activity where children work things out together.

Resources: Planks, ropes, large boxes, tubes, crates, logs, sticks, bamboo, material, large plastic sheets.

How? Encourage children to build shelters, vehicles, balancing equipment, anything that goes with their role play. Help them with fixing things together, ask them 'how can we do that?' 'What do you need?'. Encourage them to draw their construction before or afterwards.

Helpful hint: Draw their attention to how they get things to balance, find things the same length, need something longer or shorter. Have large sheets of paper available for them to draw their plans.

Under 2s: Collect smaller, lighter boxes (shoe boxes) and blocks and help them build. Count blocks as they build; let them knock their building down as this is great fun! 1, 2, 3...Go!

IDEA! Number your wheeled toys and parking bays so children have to match them up to park their cars, scooters and bikes. Ride wheeled toys through water and make shapes and patterns on the ground.

Activity 11: Tidying up! Sorting, counting, recording (2-5s)

Why? This is a great way to tidy up! Or pretend you need to tidy up! It is purposeful, fun and active.

Resources: 3 or 4 boxes/containers, different toys such as balls, bean bags, stones, plastic plates etc, dolls, anything!

How? The idea is to sort the toys out into the various containers. There are different ways to use this idea. Place the toys in the middle with the containers a short distance away in different corners. Children are responsible for tidying one set of toys into one container. Two or three children can work together as a team. They can do this by: Doing it as fast as they can. See who finishes first.

Then ask them to count what is in their container. Asking children to run and fetch 2/3/4 objects at a time. You could also ask all children to tidy up everything, putting things into the right containers, so they run around more.

Helpful hint: Have number cards to represent the number of things they have in their containers. Have clipboards for them to tally their numbers on, making a mark for each item.

Under 2s: Encourage toddlers to put their toys into boxes. Enable non-walking children to help themselves from a box/basket of toys and put them back. This is the beginning of recognising differences in things and sorting.

Get active!

A movement approach to Mathematics

Activity 12: Using natural materials – shape, space and measure (2-5s)

Why? This is a different way of exploring shapes and being creative, and combines exploration of natural materials with understanding about shape, space and measure.

Resources: Containers with stones, gravel, sticks, shells, pine cones and anything else natural.

How? Make shapes with stones, sticks, pebbles, shells. Make long creatures – measure them. Create pathways for others to follow – ask 'how many steps to the end of your pathway?' Talk about curved and straight pathways (rather than wiggly). Make patterns, talk about these, matching bits, repeating patterns.

Helpful hint: This activity can also have a creative focus, making faces, gardens, patterns.

Under 2s: Take young children on a walk to find the natural materials. Let them play with them as they wish, filling containers, placing them inside, underneath, making lines and circles. Notice how they play, this will tell you about there thinking patterns, their schema. This develops their pre-maths skills. You may notice similar play patterns in other things they do.

IDEA! Why not ride wheeled toys through water and make shapes and patterns on the ground?

Activity 13: Chasing numbers – number recognition

Why? This is a fun active way of recognising numbers and dots on a dice.

Resources: A dice with dots or numbers, a circle of spots, seats, logs, something to sit on.

How? 6 children sit in a circle. They have a number on the ground in front of them or around their necks. A child rolls the dice and runs around the outside of the circle to change places with that number. See who sits down first! That child then rolls the dice and so on.

Helpful hint: Try both types of dice. Younger children will soon recognise the pattern and link that to the number.

Activity 14: Musical shapes/ numbers

Why? This is a fun and active way of consolidating their knowledge!

Resources: Music player and lively music.

How?
Numbers: Play the music and when it stops children join together in 2s, 3s, 4s, 5s or alone according to what you say.

Shapes: When the music stops, children make their bodies into the shape you say.

Helpful hint: Children can also work in pairs to make the shapes.

Under 2s: Play musical statues, so that children get used to stopping when the music stops. This can be developed into making a star/long/small shape with their bodies.

Get active!

A movement approach to Understanding the World

People and communities

This aspect is about learning about themselves and the people around them. Children are learning all about their bodies and how they interact with the world when they are active and as they grow and develop. They learn how their bodies work and how to take care of themselves. Many physical games are social and help children learn about others. It is also about recognising similarities and differences between themselves and others. As they play with each other, they learn about differences in ages and physical abilities, and they learn that not all children enjoy doing the same things. They learn which children are fearless and those who are more wary.

Activity	Adult role
Climbing and balancing Locomotor and ball games	Encourage children to watch each other, to comment on achievements, to notice who is younger and older and what they can do. Talk about what they like to do and what other children enjoy.

The world

This aspect is about understanding the natural and man-made world around them and exploring the different features. Outdoors is a great place for physical activity. As children use both natural and man-made features of the outdoors for climbing and balancing like trees, tyres, rocks and walls they find out about their properties. They learn that a tree trunk wobbles when they walk on it, and has bark that peals off, that they can hide beneath the leafy branches, that tyres are bouncy, that rocks are hard, sometimes smooth and sometimes jagged. As they ride wheeled toys they learn about road layouts and safety. When they climb high they can spot shapes in the environment, they can see things are smaller from a distance.

Technology

This aspect is about using technology for particular purposes. Children learn to use music players as they dance around. They can use timers as they play games and try to 'beat the clock' or improve their 'record'. Chasing after remote-controlled cars is a great physical activity!

Expressive movement is an ideal medium for helping children to understand so much about their world. Any theme can be translated into movement. For example, they can learn about under the sea, machines, different feelings, animals and insects. (See Section 3)

Activity	Adult role
Climbing on natural features	Encourage children to notice details about the natural world, the roughness of a log, how grass becomes muddy.
Using man-made equipment	Explore and talk about how tyres roll, notice how portable climbing equipment fixes together.
Wheeled toys	Set up road signs and traffic control. Help children to play together and learn when to stop at traffic lights, wait for people to cross the road, give way at the roundabout etc.

Get active!

A movement approach to Expressive Arts and Design

Exploring and using media and materials

A large part of this area of learning is about moving to different sounds and music, which is covered thoroughly in Section 3: Movement and Dance. As well as dancing, It is about learning rhymes and songs, which can be done in a very active and physical way.

The other aspect of this area is experimenting and being creative with different materials and tools. Children learn about textures and how different materials behave as they play with movement play materials (elastics, scarves and Lycra). Large-scale construction play gives children experiences of using different tools for cutting and fixing things, as well as the physical lifting and carrying. Art on a big scale has great opportunities for creativity as well as being a whole body activity.

Being Imaginative

This aspect is about children using their knowledge of media and materials imaginatively in design and technology, art, music, dance, role play and stories. Many activities have already been covered, in movement and dance, and examples of creating large scale construction and art above. A particularly exciting activity is adventure role play. This is action-packed role play on a grand scale, both imaginative and very physical.

Activity	Adult role
Movement play	Draw children's attention to the 'stretchiness' of the Lycra, the softness of other materials in the movement area, how elastic stretches.
Large-scale construction	See Maths Activity 11. Help children solve problems about what to use to fix things together, string, rope, pegs, hooks, tape. Ask 'is that strong enough?' As they get older, ask them to plan what they want to make, making a drawing or talking it through. With younger children, talk about 'sticky' with tape and 'snap' with pegs.
Large-scale art	Use sheets, wall paper and large pieces of plastic for painting. This becomes a very physical activity. Do foot and hand print painting big style.
Adventure role play	Provide climbing areas and loose building equipment for use as a pirate ship, fire station or super-hero base. Allow children to play actively and jump from steps into the sea, slide down fire poles, and balance along planks in the jungle. Older children could re-tell their stories to the group, or create their own 'story books'.
Purposeful bikes!	Have 2 or 3 areas for role play that children can move between on their 'transport', for example, a garage, a home, shop, a hospital, a fire station.
Create outdoor sculptures	Use recyclable and natural materials to create large outdoor sculptures.

Working with parents and carers

If parents and carers know and understand the value of movement play, the importance of developing locomotor, balance and ball skills, and how children learn best in a physical way, the impact of your work will be much greater. They will appreciate what you are doing and will support you with similar activities at home.

They need to know:

- What movement play is, and why it is so important

- What clothing is suitable for everyday play

- How you play with the children and have bodily contact

- The 5 key movement activities essential for healthy development

- How movement play links to overall development so they can appreciate its huge importance in learning and developing

- What games you play with balls and small equipment

- The imaginative dances you are doing.

Some ideas for involving parents and carers:

- Open sessions when parents/carers can join in games with their children, supported by information about the value of movement play

- A 'Movement play policy', explaining what it is and why it is a crucial part of everyday practice

- Display photos annotating children's physical achievements and describing their movements

- Activity bags to take home, supported by a play session

- Use your website, newsletter or Facebook page, if you have one, to let parents/carers know the games you play at the nursery so they can play them at home with their children.

Planning for everyone

Planning for physical development is the same as planning for other areas. The same principles apply! Effective planning is likely to include:

- The Characteristics of Effective Learning (see Section 4)

- Clear learning intentions based on observations, for example, 'to develop and practice different movement skills of hopping, jumping, running and encourage children to be energetic'

- Description of the activity i.e. what the children are expected/likely to do, what the adult is expected to do, the environment

- Key vocabulary and questions to be used, for example, If challenging children on the climbing frame, or during movement sessions, For example, 'can you get around the climbing frame without using your knees?'. 'Can you balance on 3 different parts of your body at the same time?'

- The role of the adult, to teach, support, encourage children to: 'be energetic', 'balance on different parts of their bodies', 'approach the climbing frame from different directions', and 'throw at a target'

- Resources and how these may be combined or adapted

- How to extend and adapt activities/equipment/teaching to meet the needs of all children (see below)

- Assessment opportunities (if appropriate)

- Sometimes, themes such as: balancing and stretching, under and over, zigzag pathways. You could arrange equipment indoors/outdoors using a theme to encourage children to use equipment in particular ways

- Risk assessment where appropriate

- Evaluation of how the activities went, and what could be improved next time and individual achievements.

Remember: You won't have to do this every time, plans will often be reusable as you will often have the same learning intention for example, 'throwing skills with 3/4 year olds', 'climbing equipment outdoors/indoors'. Just adapt them to meet the needs of the group.

Ensure inclusion

When planning a session, you should think how all children can be successful and feel good about their achievements.

Physical development is all about finding out what your body can do and this is different for each child. Careful consideration should be given to individual children and different groups of children so that all children enjoy and benefit from physical play.

Remember they are all working towards the same goals; they are just at different stages in Early Years Outcomes.

You need to consider younger and older children, boys and girls, timid and bold children, children learning English, children with special educational needs that may include:

- Physical disabilities

- Learning difficulties

- Emotional problems

- Dyspraxia

- Challenging behaviour.

Planning needs to include the following:

- Equipment so it is challenging for the different abilities

- Activities so all children can join in

- How you teach and support children so that each child can understand and respond in their own way.

Build on individual learning programmes. Enlist extra staff support.

Playing safely

Risk and challenge are key factors in developing children's confidence and willingness to 'have a go' at new and different activities; this is how they learn and develop resilience.

Being able to make decisions about risk and challenge in childhood is vital to developing healthy future attitudes to choices in life. It is your role to provide a safe environment where children can take manageable risks and challenge

themselves both physically and intellectually. Children can only develop their own understanding of risk by taking risks within a well organised and safe environment.

Talking about their choices plays a key role in children's growing ability to make informed decisions about when to take a risk. Asking questions will make children think through consequences and what will happen if...For example, 'what will happen if you jump from this platform?' How will you get down when you are at the top?' What will happen if more than 2 children stand on this plank?' This is preparing them for life experiences!

Your role, therefore, is to enable children to make their own decisions about what is safe to try. Even the youngest children can work out if they can crawl over a door frame, or onto the grass, if you have risk assessed the areas accurately.

Reflection

Review your risk assessment system.
Have you removed equipment for safety reasons?
Could it still be used if it is made safer?
What risks can children take safely?
How well do you encourage children to assess what is risky?

Health and Safety Policy: Risk assessments

Your risk assessment policy and procedures should cover the general use, and wear and tear of your large and small physical play equipment, and your indoor and outdoor spaces.

Daily risk assessments

Climbing and balancing equipment

On a daily basis, when combining different pieces of large equipment, to provide challenging and creative climbing and balancing experiences, consider how safe this is for children's use. This will entail looking at:

■ The suitability of the ground surface

■ The space around it, closeness to other play areas

■ The connections between the separate pieces of equipment

■ The suitability for the children of different ages, sizes and stages of development

■ The staff supervision.

New games and activities

When trying out new games and activities, have a risk assessment section in your planning. Consider:

■ Space

■ Use of equipment

■ Ground surface

■ Supervision/adult role

■ Children's different ages and stages of physical development

■ Any additional needs.

Have a positive, 'can do' approach to risk assessment. For example, how can we make the climbing frame more challenging? How can we make the steps safer for the younger children? (Instead of taking them away!)

8-week Development Programme

This programme will embed a physical approach to learning and development into your setting. You will focus on a different aspect of provision each week so that you build up a physically rich environment to fully develop children's physical literacy and overall learning.

8-week Development Programme for under 2s

Week	Adult role	Get active!
Week 1 Focus: Movement Play Proprioception Movement area	**Read Section 1: Movement Play and complete the 'Reflection' activities.** **Observe** your key children's stages of development and note what they can do and are likely to do next. **Get down on the floor** and play with the children, **encourage back and tummy play** using your body as a climbing frame.	Set up **a movement area**. Look at the whole room and **everyday practice** in terms of a **'movement friendly environment'**. Provide **resources for back and tummy play**, body balls etc. Make sure **'waiting times'** at meal times are absolutely minimal.
Review	**What worked well?**	**What can you improve? How?** **Complete the 'Equipment review sheet' on page 75.**
Week 2 Focus: Movement Play Vestibular development *And* Review climbing and balancing	**Complete the 'Revision of key knowledge' on pages 77 and 79.** **Note** your key children's development over the previous week, and how you have encouraged this (record). Continue with your **'body play'**. Notice what each child prefers in the way of movement play, and spend prolonged periods playing. Introduce **rocking and spinning** movements with children in your arms and notice their responses. Review children's **climbing and balancing** experiences.	Enhance your **movement area** with different materials, equipment and music etc. to promote **spinning, tipping and tilting** (vestibular development). Use the Lycra for **rocking** babies, encourage them to **roll** on soft surfaces and sloping equipment. List the **climbing equipment** you have indoors and outdoors and record: ■ How often it is used ■ Who uses it ■ What skills they practise.
Review	**What worked well?**	**What can you improve? How?**

8-week Development Programme for under 2s

Week	Adult role	Get active!
Week 3 Focus: Climbing and balancing *Continue* Movement play *And* Review ball skills	**Read Section 2: Movement Skills, and complete the 'Reflection' activities.** Encourage children to use different **climbing and balancing** equipment indoors and outdoors. Continue with **movement play**, as an everyday part of every child's experiences.	Improve **climbing and balancing** experiences, based on your review of equipment and its use. **Rearrange** your existing climbing and balancing equipment to make it more challenging, both indoors and outdoors. Make a wish list! List the equipment you have for developing **ball skills** and record: ■ How often it is used ■ Who uses it ■ How they are used.
Review	**What worked well?**	**What can you improve? How?** **Complete the 'Equipment review sheet' on page 75.**
Week 4 Focus: Ball skills *Continue* Movement play Improving climbing experiences	**Complete the 'Revision of key knowledge' on pages 78 and 80.** Introduce **ball play**, at the level of your key children. Rolling balls to them, encouraging **rolling, throwing and kicking**. Continue with **movement play** as everyday practice, providing lots of experiences for proprioceptive and vestibular development. Encourage children to try new experiences **climbing and balancing.**	Make sure you have a **variety of soft balls, covered balloons and bean bags**, which are attractive to children. Use the body balls, bouncers, Lycra and scarves and keep improving your Movement Play area. **Combine equipment** together in different ways to provide a variety of pathways for getting on and off.
Review	**What worked well?**	**What can you improve? How?**

8-week Development Programme for under 2s

Week	Adult role	Get active!
Week 5 Focus: Overall provision!	Continue with **movement play** as everyday practice. Get to know the children's preferences, and provide what their bodies and minds need!	Provide **movement play** and exciting **climbing and balancing** experiences daily. Provide **ball play** experiences according to children's interests, and at least **3 times a week**. Have balls easily accessible to choose any time.
Review	**What worked well?**	**What can you improve? How?**
Week 6 Focus: Movement and Dance *Continue* Good daily practice	**Read Section 3: Movement and Dance (in relation to younger children) and complete the 'Reflection' activity.** Find a new rhyme on a website or on YouTube. As children are playing, sing songs that go with their play, such as *Old MacDonald had a Farm*.	**Jig about** to lively music with babies in your arms twice a day. Try different types of music from different countries. **Use streamers, scarves, ribbon sticks.** Introduce the **new rhyme** to children and sing it every day. Have a **regular rhyme time** with lots of **whole body** action songs.
Review	**What worked well?**	**What can you improve? How?**

8-week Development Programme for under 2s

Week	Adult role	Get active!
Week 7 Focus: Movement and the Curriculum Communication and Language, Literacy and Mathematics *Continue* Good daily practice	**Read Section 4: A Movement approach to learning, and complete the 'Reflection' activity on the Characteristics of Effective Learning.** Choose 2 new activities each day from the Get active! for Communication and Language, Literacy, and Mathematics.	Give **words to children's actions; bring stories to life** by making them more physical; **comment on the sound** of the instruments they play. At this stage in the programme, you will already be playing with balls and moving up and down climbing equipment with toddlers. Focus on the **maths language** of up, down, inside and out, through and **Count 123**...Go! Jump! Run! count to 3 with body actions (jumps, claps).
Review	**What worked well?**	**What can you improve? How?**
Week 8 Focus: Movement and the Curriculum Understanding the World, Expressive Arts and Design	This is about doing the same activities, like dancing, rolling on the floor, clambering and emphasising different learning aspects of Understanding the world, and Expressive arts and design. It's all about your interaction. **Complete the 'Revision of key knowledge' on page 82.**	Comment on what children **like to do and don't like to do**. Encourage them to **watch and communicate** with each other. Help children to **notice how the natural world feels**; give them words to connect with their physical body experience, such as soft, hard, rough, prickly. How much of the natural world is available for your group of children? Can you improve this? Focus on the **Movement and Dance** Section 3 again. Make your art activities **whole body experiences,** such as foot and hand print painting, custard play.
Review	**What worked well?**	**What can you improve? How?**

Prime Time **PHYSICAL**

8-week Development Programme for 2-3s

Week	Adult role	Get active!
Week 1 Focus: Movement Play Proprioception Movement area	**Read Section 1: Movement Play, and complete the 'Reflection' activities**. **Observe** your key children's stages of development and note what they can do and are likely to do next. **Get down on the floor** and play with the children. Let them squirm through your legs, under a bridge. Encourage **back and tummy play**. Develop an atmosphere of respect for movement. Become used to bodily contact. Establish **movement play rules**.	Set up a **movement area** (See guidance in Section 1). Look at the whole room and everyday practice in terms of a **'movement friendly environment'**. Can some activities be done more comfortably on the floor? Set up painting and drawing activities on the floor. Provide resources for **back and tummy play**, body balls etc. Make sure **'waiting times'** at meal times are absolutely minimal.
Review	**What worked well?**	**What can you improve? How?**
Week 2 Focus: Movement Play Vestibular development *Introduce:* Movement games (locomotor) *and* Review climbing and balancing	**Complete the 'Revision of key knowledge' on pages 77 and 79**. **Note** your key children's development over the previous week, and how you have encouraged this (record). Continue with your **'body play'**. Notice what each child prefers in the way of movement play, and spend longer periods playing. Introduce **pulling and pushing** movements with a tug of war. Develop **rocking and spinning** movements. Lead simple **movement games.** Review **climbing and balancing** experiences.	Enhance your **movement area** with different materials, equipment and music etc. to promote **spinning, tipping and tilting**. Use the Lycra for a tug of war, and for spinning children round. Encourage them to roll on soft surfaces and sloping equipment. Play a simple **movement game** every day such as 'follow the leader', musical statues, the Bean game. Use rhymes to encourage **rocking and spinning**, such as, 'Teddy Bear, Teddy Bear turn around', 'Row, row row the boat'. List the **climbing equipment** you have indoors and outdoors and record: ■ How often it is used ■ Who uses it ■ What skills they practise.
Review	**What worked well?**	**What can you improve? How?** **Complete the 'Equipment review sheet' on page 75.**

8-week Development Programme for 2-3s

Week	Adult role	Get active!
Week 3 Focus: Climbing and balancing *Continue* Movement play *And* Review ball skills	**Read Section 2: Movement Skills and complete the 'Reflection' activities.** Encourage them to use different **climbing and balancing** equipment indoors and outdoors. Continue with **movement play** as an everyday part of every child's experiences. Lead simple **movement games for running and jumping**, such as follow the leader, rhymes, the Bean game.	Improve **climbing and balancing** experiences, based on your review of equipment and its use. Be creative with what you have! Think of under, over, round and through. **Rearrange** your existing equipment to make it more challenging, both indoors and outdoors. Make a wish list! Play simple **movement games** as in week 2. List the equipment you have for developing **ball skills** and record: ■ How often it is used ■ Who uses it ■ How they are used.
Review	**What worked well?**	**What can you improve? How?** **Complete the 'Equipment review sheet' on page 75.**
Week 4 Focus: Ball skills *Continue* Movement play Movement games Improving climbing experiences	**Complete the 'Revision of key knowledge' on pages 78 and 80.** Introduce **ball play**, focus on **throwing and kicking** at the level of your key children. Continue with **movement play** every day, emphasising proprioceptive and vestibular development. Play **simple games** spontaneously as week 3. Encourage children to try new experiences **climbing and balancing**.	Make sure you have variety of **soft balls and bean bags**, which are attractive to children. Introduce **simple games** using targets and buckets to throw at and into. Use the body balls and Lycra and **keep improving your movement play area**, adding music, scarves and ribbon sticks. **Combine** equipment in different ways to provide variety of pathways for approaching equipment.
Review	**What worked well?**	**What can you improve? How?**

8-week Development Programme for 2-3s

Week	Adult role	Get active!
Week 5 Focus: Overall provision!	Support **movement play, climbing and balancing and ball play** as everyday practice. Get to know the children's preferences, and provide what their bodies and minds need!	Provide daily **movement play**, exciting **climbing and balancing experiences**. Provide **ball play** experiences according to children's interests, and at least 3 times a week. Always have them easily accessible for free choice.
Review	What worked well?	What can you improve? How?
Week 6 Focus: Movement and Dance *Continue* Good daily practice	**Read Section 3: Movement and Dance (in relation to younger children) and complete the 'Reflection' activity and the 'Revision of key knowledge' on page 81**. Learn a new rhyme. Use YouTube. As children are playing, sing songs that go with their play, such as *Old MacDonald had a Farm*.	**Jig about** to lively music with children twice a day, Section 3 (Activity 7) Try different types of music from different countries. **Use streamers, scarves, ribbon sticks.** **Try 1 activity a day** from Section 3, using ideas children are familiar with, like pretending to be different animals or the weather. Introduce a **new rhyme** to children and sing it every day. Have a **regular rhyme time** with lots of **whole body** action songs.
Review	What worked well?	What can you improve? How?

8-week Development Programme for 2-3s

Week	Adult role	Get active!
Week 7 Focus: Movement and the Curriculum Communication and Language, Literacy and Mathematics *Continue* Good daily practice	**Read Section 4: Movement and the Curriculum, and complete the 'Reflection' activity on the Characteristics of Effective Learning.** Choose 2 new activities from Section 4: Get active! each day from the programme for Communication and language, Literacy, and Mathematics.	Follow the guidance for language activities. Give **words to children's actions; go big** on action rhymes, **bring stories to life** by making them more physical; **comment on the sound** of the instruments they play. At this stage in the programme, you will already be playing with balls and moving up and down climbing equipment with children. Focus on the **maths language** of up, down, inside and out, through. **Count steps, count the skittles and balls in the box!**
Review	**What worked well?**	**What can you improve? How?**
Week 8 Focus: Movement and the Curriculum Understanding the World, Expressive Arts and Design	This is about doing the same activities, like dancing, movement play, clambering and emphasising different learning aspects of Understanding the world and Expressive arts and design. It's all about your interaction. **Complete the 'Revision of key knowledge' on page 82.**	Comment on what children **like to do and don't like to do**. Encourage them to **watch and communicate** with each other. Help children to **notice how the natural world feels**; give them words to connect with their physical body experience, such as soft, hard, rough, prickly. How much of the natural world is available for your group of children? Can you improve this? Focus on the **Movement and Dance** Section 3 again. Make your art activities **whole body experiences**, such as foot and hand print painting.
Review	**What worked well?**	**What can you improve? How?**

PHOTOCOPIABLE

8-week Development Programme for 3-5s

Week	Adult role	Get active!
Week 1 Focus: Movement Play Proprioception Movement area	**Read Section 1: Movement Play, and complete the 'Reflection' activities.** **Observe** your key children's stages of development and note what they can do and are trying to achieve. **Get down on the floor** and play with the children. Let them squirm through your legs, under a bridge. Develop an atmosphere of respect for movement. Become used to bodily contact. Establish **movement play rules**.	Set up a **movement area**. Look at the whole room and everyday practice in terms of a **'movement friendly environment'**. Are there any activities that can be done more comfortably on the floor? Set up writing, painting and drawing activities on the floor. Use imaginative ideas for floor play – moving like snakes, caterpillars, swimming, roll over sideways. Provide resources for **back and tummy play** such as body balls, soft play. Make sure **'waiting times'** at meal times, going outdoors and other 'routine' times are absolutely minimal.
Review	**What worked well?**	**What can you improve? How?**
Week 2 Focus: Movement Play Vestibular development *Introduce* Movement games *And* Review climbing and balancing	**Complete the 'Revision of key knowledge' on pages 77 and 79.** **Note** your key children's development over the previous week, and how you have encouraged this (record). Continue with your **'body play'**. Notice what each child prefers in the way of movement play, and spend longer periods playing. Introduce **pulling and pushing movements** with a tug of war. Support **rocking, rolling, spinning**. Review **climbing and balancing** experiences.	Enhance your **movement area** with different materials, equipment, music etc. to promote **spinning, tipping, tilting**. Use the Lycra for a tug of war, for spinning children round, scarves and ribbon sticks for twirling. Encourage them to **roll and spin** on soft surfaces. Use music for dancing. Introduce **a movement game** every day such as 'follow the leader', 'musical statues', 'the Bean game', try 'Corners' focusing on different types of animal movements. (Section 2 Activities). List the **climbing equipment** you have indoors and outdoors and record: ■ How often it is used ■ Who uses it ■ How they are used.
Review	**What worked well?**	**What can you improve? How?** **Complete the 'Equipment review sheet' on page 75.**

8-week Development Programme for 3-5s

Week	Adult role	Get active!
Week 3 Focus: Climbing and balancing *Continue* Movement play Movement games *And* Review ball skills	**Read Section 2: Movement skills, and complete the 'Reflection' activities**. Encourage them to use different **climbing and balancing** equipment indoors and outdoors. Use a problem solving approach as you interact to challenge children's skills. Continue with **movement play**, as an everyday part of every child's experiences.	Improve **climbing and balancing** experiences, based on your review of equipment and its use. **Rearrange** your existing equipment to make it more challenging, both indoors and outdoors. Be creative! Put equipment together in new ways! Make a wish list! Play simple **movement games** every day as week 2, introducing the 'lifeboats' game. List the equipment you have for developing **ball skills** and record: ■ How often it is used ■ Who uses it ■ How they are used.
Review	**What worked well?**	**What can you improve? How?** **Complete the 'Equipment review sheet' on page 75.**
Week 4 Focus: Ball skills *Continue* Movement play Improving climbing experiences	**Complete the 'Revision of key knowledge' on pages 78 and 80.** **Introduce ball play**, focus on **throwing and kicking** at the level of your key children. Notice what stage they are at in their skill development, and provide the right support at the right time. Continue with **movement play** every day, emphasising proprioceptive and vestibular development. Encourage children to challenge themselves on the **large equipment**. Use a problem solving approach in your encouragement.	Make sure you have **a variety of soft balls and bean bags**, which are attractive to children. Introduce simple games using targets, cones, hoops and buckets, with a focus on throwing, kicking and dribbling skills. Choose a different game each day from Section 2. **Combine climbing and balancing equipment** in different ways to provide a variety of pathways for getting on and off.
Review	**What worked well?**	**What can you improve? How?**

PHOTOCOPIABLE

Prime Time **PHYSICAL**

8-week Development Programme for 3-5s

Week	Adult role	Get active!
Week 5 Focus: Overall provision!	Continue with **movement play** as everyday practice. Get to know the children's preferences, and provide what their bodies and minds need!	**Provide daily movement play, exciting climbing and balancing experiences, movement games and ball play.** Set up an area indoors or outdoors every day for target throwing, rolling or kicking according to children's interests, ensuring you cover all the ball skills over the week.
Review	**What worked well?**	**What can you improve? How?**
Week 6 Focus: Movement and Dance *Continue* Good daily practice	**Read Section 3: Movement and Dance and complete the 'Reflection' activity and the 'Revision of key knowledge' on page 81.** Work out a simple exercise routine to music. Find out what your children are interested in this week, what is their role play about? **Observe and record children's developing physical skills.**	**Lead a short movement/dance session every day.** Begin with **exercises to music** (2 days). Use different levels, remember sitting exercises. Try a movement session based on what your children are interested in, such as animals, fish, castles, or superheroes (2 days). See ideas in Section 4. Day 5 is your or the children's choice! **Provide daily movement play, climbing and balancing, movement games and ball play** (as week 5).
Review	**What worked well?**	**What can you improve? How?**

8-week Development Programme for 3-5s

Week	Adult role	Get active!
Week 7 Focus: Movement and the Curriculum **Communication and Language, Literacy and Mathematics**	Read Section 4: Movement and the Curriculum, and complete the 'Reflection' activity on the Characteristics of Effective Learning. **Choose 2 new activities each day for Communication and Language, Literacy, and Mathematics.**	**Give words to children's actions**, encouraging them to use movement language. Tell a story using movement; choose a book children know well. Choose a literacy activity from Section 4. At this stage in the programme, your movement and ball games will be well established. **Focus on counting** as you play target and running games. Introduce **3 new games** to do this week.
Review	**What worked well?**	**What can you improve? How?**
Week 8 Focus: Movement and the Curriculum Understanding the World, Expressive Arts and Design	This is about doing the same activities, like dancing, movement play, locomotor and ball games, climbing and balancing and emphasising different aspects of Understanding the World and Expressive Arts and Design. It is all about your interaction. **Complete the 'Revision of key knowledge' on page 82.**	Encourage children to **notice and value each other's achievements** and to **respect** each other's **preferred activities**. Draw their attention to the natural world as they play on trees, rocks and grass. **Focus on Movement and Dance Section 3 again**, choose 3 new sessions, prompting further understanding of their world. **Encourage adventure play**, plan for **large scale construction** and **art**.
Review	**What worked well?**	**What can you improve? How?**

Week 5 (All ages)

This is the week where you review practice, ask yourself 'where are we now?' and plan ahead.

As a team, discuss the changes you have made and the new activities you have introduced over the past 5 weeks. Record what has worked well, what you would change, and what you would still like to improve. Research equipment issues.

Your everyday practice and nursery ethos for physical development should now be well-established, with all staff having a positive approach to physical play, knowledgeable and comfortable with movement play, and enjoying leading daily movement games.

The key to continued good practice is to constantly observe your children's physical achievements and what they are trying to do. Then base your planning for the environment, equipment and activities on this essential knowledge.

Week 5 (All ages)

Planning guidance

Make physical development a significant part of your overall planning

Movement play

This should be well-established now. Monitor how children use the movement area, how staff feel about it, and adapt and enhance accordingly.

Climbing and balancing

Each week review the layout of your equipment and think how it can be changed to be more challenging to meet the needs of your children.

Locomotor movement games

Plan fun games every day and play active games spontaneously indoors/outdoors. Have small equipment readily available for children to plan their own games.

Ball games

Set up games daily for older children. Have a wide variety of attractive balls and bean bags to throw, roll, catch, kick and strike. Make these constantly accessible.

Overall review and future plans

Provision	Changes	What works well Why?	What does not work well, Why?	Improvements, When? Who?
Movement play				
Climbing and balancing				
Movement skills/games				
Ball skills/games				
Movement and dance				
A movement approach to learning				

What it's all about!

The Prime Time Physical Programme is about the impact on children. Choose 2 children and describe the progress and changes in their development.

Child, age, obs context	PSED	Language	Physical development	Overall improvements

PHOTOCOPIABLE

Equipment review sheet (Programme weeks 2 & 3)

	Resources available	Resources needed
General resources for movement play Body ball, cushions, streamers, ribbons, scarves, soft play, mats, Lycra etc.		
Resources for climbing and balancing, hanging and swinging		
Resources for ball play Different sized balls, bean bags, soft toys to throw, targets, cones, hoops, skittles, bats and sticks.		

Revision of key knowledge

Use this document throughout the 8-week programme to help you consolidate your knowledge and reflect on practice.

Revision of key knowledge

Think about babies and young children for each type of movement, describe the kind of activities you provide and the parts of the body and senses that these strengthen and support.

Back play and tummy play	Belly crawling	Crawling

Spin, tip, tilt	Push, pull, stretch, hang	Movement play
		List some points you might make to parents to explain the importance of child-led, adult-supported movement play.

Basic movement skills (what the body does)

Basic movement skills are the movements a child is physically ready to develop and refine during the early years.

LOCOMOTOR SKILLS Moving from A to B	BALANCE SKILLS Balancing the body in stillness and in motion	BALL SKILLS Send, receive, travel, strike

Revision of key knowledge

Movement Play: Section 1 (weeks 1 and 2)

What is developmental movement?

What is movement play? Why is it important?

What are proprioception and vestibular development?

What are the 5 key movement activities for children's healthy development?

Revision of key knowledge

Movement Skills: Section 2 (weeks 3 and 4)

What are movement skills?

How can you categorise them into 3 areas?

What are the 3 stages of skill development?

How should you use this knowledge?

Revision of key knowledge

Movement and Dance: Section 3 (week 6)

What are movement concepts?

Why are they important?

How do they develop?

Draw the Movement Effort Graph

How can this help you when leading movement and dance sessions?

Revision of key knowledge

Movement and the Curriculum: Section 4 (weeks 7 and 8)

Why is it important to have a movement approach to learning?

What are the Characteristics of Effective Learning? Why is it important to use these as a basis for planning?

Audit

Use this audit before and after you do the 8-week programme. This will highlight areas you are already doing well and those that you can develop.

Audit

0-2 years

This audit will enable you to track your progress with the Prime Time Physical 8-week programme, before you start it and at the end. It will identify the strengths in your setting and where you can improve children's physical experiences.

Questions	Established	Developing	Not yet in place	Action	Date
STAFF ATTITUDES					
Do you all have a positive approach to children's movement?					
Do you all value and encourage children's natural movement play?					
Do you all use positive language when children are naturally energetic?					
Do you all use the language of movement to develop children's vocabulary?					
Do you all encourage children to take manageable risks?					
CHILDREN					
Do 0-2s move smoothly from one activity to another with as little 'waiting' time as possible?					
Do 0-2s have the floor space to crawl, wriggle and roll?					
Do 0-2s spend time on their tummies and backs, use a body ball and other soft play equipment for tummy & back play?					
Do 0-2s crawl & climb on, over, through & round a range of climbing equipment?					
Do 0-2s play with a range of soft balls of different sizes?					
Do toddlers clamber on a range of climbing and balancing equipment?					
Do 0-2s use you as a climbing frame?					
Do 0-2s enjoy being rocked, and playing upside down, swinging & spinning games with you?					

PHOTOCOPIABLE

Prime Time **PHYSICAL**

Audit

0-2 years

Questions	Established	Developing	Not yet in place	Action	Date
CHILDREN					
Do 0-2s enjoy you playing alongside on the floor, mirroring their crawling and commando crawling, having races, and chasing games?					
Do 0-2s play with pushing and pulling toys and play gentle games?					
Do 0-2s listen to music at certain times for a purpose? Do you limit background music?					
Do 0-2s enjoy jigging about with you to music?					
Do 0-2s have a regular rhyme time?					
Do 0-2s learn new rhymes, make rhymes active, sing spontaneously with you when they play?					
Do children learn to count as they get ready to throw/run/crawl?					
Do 0-2s enjoy stories when you emphasise sounds and actions?					
PLANNING & OBSERVATION					
Do you note children's physical development and use this to plan?					
Do you include what you are doing for physical development in your written plans?					
Do you review and evaluate practice?					
Have you worked through the 8-week programme?					

Audit

2-3 years

Questions	Established	Developing	Not yet in place	Action	Date
STAFF ATTITUDES					
Do you all have a positive approach to children's movement?					
Do you all value and encourage children's natural movement play?					
Do you all use positive language when children are naturally energetic?					
Do you all use the language of movement to develop children's vocabulary?					
Do you all encourage children to take manageable risks?					
CHILDREN					
Do children move smoothly from one activity to another with as little 'waiting' time as possible?					
Do children move easily around the room; have you created good spaces?					
Do children lie on their tummies to play, build, draw and paint? Do you organise activities on the floor?					
Do children play in a movement area, with body ball, Lycra, music, streamers etc? Please describe the area.					
Do children rock, swing, twirl, and turn upside down, with your help?					
Do children play pushing and pulling games?					
Do children use you as a climbing frame as you play with them on the floor?					
Do children play with a range of soft balls of different sizes?					
Do children roll, kick and throw balls in simple target games organised by you?					
Do children practise jumping, running and stopping in games like the Bean game, Mr Wolf, musical statues, games with cones and hoops?					
Do children dance to a range of music from around the world?					

Audit

2-3 years

Questions	Established	Developing	Not yet in place	Action	Date
CHILDREN					
Do children take part in simple 'let's pretend' movement sessions, such as being animals?					
Do children learn to count, use positional language & recognise shapes as they climb and play games?					
Do children bring a simple story to life through movement?					
Do children notice other children's achievements, encouraged by you?					
Do children do large-scale art and sensory play?					
Do children know lots of rhymes, make rhymes active big-style, and sing spontaneously when they play?					
PLANNING & OBSERVATION					
Do you note children's physical development and use this to plan?					
Do you include what you are doing for physical development in your written plans?					
Do you review and evaluate practice?					
Have you worked through the 8-week programme?					

Audit

3-5 years

Questions	Established	Developing	Not yet in place	Action	Date
STAFF ATTITUDES					
Do you all have a positive approach to children's movement?					
Do you all value and encourage children's natural movement play?					
Do you all use positive language when children are naturally energetic?					
Do you all use the language of movement to develop children's vocabulary?					
Do you all encourage children to take manageable risks?					
CHILDREN					
Do children move smoothly from one activity to another with as little 'waiting' time as possible?					
Do children move easily around the room; have you created good spaces?					
Do children lie on their tummies to play, build, draw and paint? Do you organise activities on the floor?					
Do children play in a movement area, with body ball, Lycra, music, streamers etc? Please describe the area.					
Do children rock, swing, twirl, and turn upside down, with your help?					
Do children play pushing and pulling games?					
Do children use you as a climbing frame as you play with them on the floor?					
Do children play with a range of soft balls of different sizes?					
Do children roll, kick and throw balls in simple target games organised by you?					
Do children practise jumping, running and stopping in games like the Bean game, Mr Wolf, musical statues, games with cones and hoops?					
Do children dance to a range of music from around the world?					

PHOTOCOPIABLE

Prime Time **PHYSICAL**

Audit

3-5 years

Questions	Established	Developing	Not yet in place	Action	Date
CHILDREN					
Do children take part in simple 'let's pretend' movement sessions, such as being animals?					
Do children learn to count, use positional language & recognise shapes as they climb and play games?					
Do children bring a simple story to life through movement?					
Do children notice other children's achievements, encouraged by you?					
Do children do large-scale art and sensory play?					
Do children know lots of rhymes, make rhymes active big-style, and sing spontaneously when they play?					
PLANNING & OBSERVATION					
Do you note children's physical development and use this to plan?					
Do you include what you are doing for physical development in your written plans?					
Do you review and evaluate practice?					
Have you worked through the 8-week programme?					

Audit   Manager

Questions	Established	Developing	Not yet in place	Action	Date
Does the Prime Time Physical programme have high priority in your setting?					
Do you have a notice board for Prime Time Physical?					
Are you familiar with the 8-week programme?					
Do you meet with key members of staff to monitor progress and support their work?					
Do you allow staff time to develop the Prime Time Physical programme?					
Do you provide a slot at staff meetings for staff to discuss and further the programme?					
Do you monitor how practice is improving in each room?					
Do you check plans to see how practice is being carried out?					
Have you purchased any new equipment to help develop the programme?					
Do you know what resources and equipment you need to improve practice in each room?					
What are the key strengths of the Prime Time Physical programme in your nursery?					
What are the areas for improvement for the Prime Time Physical programme?					

 Prime Time PHYSICAL